THE PROFESSOR BUSINESS
A Teaching Primer for Faculty

by

Barbara J. Flood
Joy K. Moll

 Learned Information, Inc.
Medford, New Jersey

Manufactured in the United States of America

Learned Information, Inc.
143 Old Marlton Pike
Medford, NJ 08055

Library of Congress Cataloging-in-Publication Data

Flood, Barbara.
    The professor business: a teaching primer for faculty/by
  Barbara J. Flood and Joy K. Moll.
        p. cm.
    Includes bibliographical references.
    ISBN 0-938734-41-5
        1. College teaching—Vocational guidance. 2. College teachers—
  In-service training. 3. Learning. I. Moll, Joy Kaiser.
  II. Title.
  LB2331.F56 1990
  378.1'25—dc20   90-32138
                                                           CIP

Cover Design by Mary McDonnell

ISBN 0-938734-41-5

It was Louis Pasteur's observation that

Chance favors the prepared mind,
But the mind does not become prepared by chance.*

*Jeremiah A. Barondess. "On Excellence." (editorial)
The Pharos 51(1):34, 1988

CONTENTS

PREFACE

This primer is the book we wish we had had when we started teaching more than two decades ago. It includes the things we wished we had known, the things nobody told us, and the things it never occurred to us would have been useful to know. It also includes new things that have affected college and university teaching during the past twenty years. It reflects our teaching experience and that of many colleagues and friends in "the professor business." It also reflects our background as information scientists interested in the communication process and the acquisition of knowledge.

This primer is intended as an overview of what we think would be helpful for the college and university teacher. Understanding the professor business requires some background knowledge of higher education. Part I provides this background with a brief historical overview, a description of some current curricular issues involving cultural ideals and values, and an explanation of the psychological factors that influence learning.

Part II presents our view of teaching as learning management. For new faculty, we have described a comprehensive model ranging from course preparation to supervision of doctoral research. The adjunct professor and the lecturer will find a variety of techniques for classroom presentation of course material. More experienced faculty will find useful hints and suggestions to expedite course revision and new course development. Administrators will find the book a useful aid for faculty development.

In addition to teaching, the professor business traditionally includes service and research. The professor serves within the college community, the professional world, and the community at large. Faculty are also scholars in their own subject disciplines. As scholars, they must keep up to date with their fields and contribute to them with research and publication of new knowledge. The professor's roles in teaching, service, and research complement and enhance each other and need to be understood in relation to each other. Part III describes these roles and how they are evaluated for reappointment, promotion, and tenure.

A note on gender designation: although the use of one gender or the other in writing is a common policy to reduce awkward constructions and make text more readable, we were uncomfortable with using just one gender for the professor. For this reason we have used the feminine gender in the first chapter, the masculine in the second, and continued to alternate gender designation for the professor, on a chapter by chapter basis, throughout the book.

Although we have based this primer on the experiences and comments of many academics, we are particularly grateful for the contributions of a few colleagues who have made especially significant contributions to the book. Mabel C. Jessee, Professor Emerita, Temple University, has been a valued supporter and critic throughout the entire writing and editing process. Donald J. Fork, U.S. Dept. of Education, helped us to sharpen our focus in several areas and provided invaluable assistance in revising our original manuscript. Esther R. Dyer, Empire Blue Cross and Blue Shield, provided both content and editorial assistance from the points of view of an academic, an administrator, and a general reader. We have come to understand why authors acknowledge and appreciate the forbearance of friends and family during the book-writing process. Ours have also been supportive and forbearing. Last, but not least, our editors at Learned Information have been a pleasure to work with. Kay Powell's insights greatly improved our original manuscript. Shirley Corsey's deftness in book production is appreciated, as is Loraine Page's copyediting and supervision of the publication process. To all—our sincere thanks.

Barbara J. Flood
Joy K. Moll
1989

Part I

Orientation to Teaching and Learning Management

Chapter 1

THE COLLEGE PROFESSOR
AS LEARNING MANAGER

Expertise in classroom teaching is essential to the professor business. It is an aspect of higher education for which the community at large is holding academia increasingly accountable. It is essential to a highly competitive, knowledge-intensive society.

Academia is a unique institution in our society. It operates under an aegis of academic freedom—the freedom of a professor to teach and research without fear and of a student to study under conditions of personal choice. The colleges and universities that constitute academia are primarily institutions of learning for professor and student alike. However, the professor's expertise also serves a wider community, being available to government, industry, and the citizenry at large.

The quintessential functions of the professor business, therefore, are teaching, research, and service to the community. The professor is expected to possess expertise in the research and needs of a particular subject area and to articulate this expertise within the academy and beyond. Indeed, the excellence of an academic institution is often equated with the level of expertise of its professors as determined by the frontiers of knowledge expanded by their research. The excellence of an academic institution, of a college or university, is less often equated with the expertise its professors demonstrate in classroom teaching. Yet, historically, teaching has always been a primary function of higher education.

The professor teaches by managing the learning experience for each student in the sense of planning and organizing a course, leading, inspiring, and encouraging critical thinking and scholarship. In the educational process, such teaching may be termed "learning management," and the professor then becomes a "learning manager." Like management in any endeavor, learning management has many facets, requires a multitude of capabilities, and is a never-ending job. It involves much more than simply communicating one's own expertise to students in a classroom, keeping up with new knowledge in the field, creating syllabi, and evaluating student progress. Ideally, the learning manager orchestrates all the activities and responsibilities that facilitate learning.

THE SPECIFIC COMPONENTS OF LEARNING MANAGEMENT

Learning management has five specific components:
1. Course planning and design
2. Presentation
3. Mentoring
4. Evaluation
5. Ongoing preparation and revision.

Suggestions for implementing these components are discussed in detail in Part II of this book. In definition and in action, some overlap among these components is inevitable.

Course planning and design entails: learning the organizational context and the environment in which the course will be taught; setting goals and objectives; and preparing a syllabus outlining the course sequence, methods of presentation and evaluation. For the new professor hired to teach existing courses in an established curriculum, concrete suggestions for course planning and design are offered in Chapter 4. Course revisions and the design of new courses are covered in Chapter 11.

The major efforts in course planning and design can seldom be completed the first time a course is offered. The feedback of the evaluation process is required for refinement. Teaching the course several times is generally necessary before the professor is satisfied with the general outline, goals and objectives, assignments, etc.

Presentation, the most detailed part of learning management, requires the professor to decide how best to present course content in the classroom, the laboratory, or in an outside assignment. The professor decides which method or methods she will be comfortable with and that will achieve the cognitive, value-related and/or performance goals set during course planning and design.

In choosing presentation methods, the professor is influenced by the particular groups of students in each class—their unique needs, interests, levels of preparation, and the social setting from which they come. Class size, availability of supplemental materials, preparation time, costs and budgets—as well as the demands of the subject matter itself—will also play a part in selecting methods.

The mentoring aspects of learning management encompass the formal and informal interactions between the professor and the class, as well as between the professor and individual students. Such efforts can be conscious or planned, such as monitoring the progress of individual students, encouraging student participation, and providing copious feedback on student assignments. Just as important, however, are such factors as the professor's enthusiasm for her subject and the desire to cultivate out-of-class contacts with students.

Many educators consider the opportunity to guide and encourage individual students the most rewarding part of teaching. Students themselves agree that they learn best with a one-to-one mentoring approach. Although the professor-student relationships formed may be temporary, they can make the student's college or university experience a positive and exciting experience. At times professors and their students form lasting friendships or collegial relationships; these can form the basis for academic and professional contacts contributing to future scholarly progress and technological development.

Evaluation of learning management includes evaluation of the student, evaluation of the course, and evaluation of the professor. Evaluation of the student includes the day-to-day monitoring of student progress in the course as well as evaluating how well the student is meeting the goals and objectives set for the course. Although students tend to equate evaluation with grades, the professor generally views evaluation more broadly. To her, evaluation also encompasses the many ways she interacts with students, hears their responses, sees what they've written on non-graded papers, etc.

The final course grade the professor gives to the student evaluates performance in only one subject area during the relatively short period of one term or semester. In assessing the long-term impact of both the professor and the course, the relevance of the grade is questionable. Unfortunately, it has a disproportionate impact at the time it is given. Such questions as how and whether the course contributed to subsequent learning, to occupational, avocational and recreational interests are ones to which the professor rarely learns the answers.

Evaluation of the course itself is extremely important to the professor as feedback and is useful for course revision. Having students evaluate a course is only part of the evaluation process, which necessarily includes assessment of one's own performance in all aspects of managing a course. Measuring quality remains a difficult and elusive task. Both faculty and administration would agree that a valid, replicable measure of course and teaching quality is a goal that has yet to be attained.

Ongoing preparation and revision reflects the faculty development increasingly emphasized by today's colleges and universities. General preparation in subject matter is usually the major criterion for hiring the new professor. The new professor has current expertise in a particular field forming part of the curricular offerings of an academic department. However, even with previous teaching experience in higher education, the new professor will often be teaching courses that must be revised and tailored to the context of a different curriculum and student body.

Experienced professors rarely offer the same course in the same way. They continually examine the planning and design process and revise the course to reflect changes in the following areas:

• *The field of study:* New developments in the field should be included in the course. This may require consolidation or even elimination of older material. A paradigm shift in the field may require adding an entirely new course, perhaps consolidating and deleting entire courses in the academic program.

• *Curricular revision:* Programs of study undergo constant change and shifting emphasis in most colleges and universities. These changes are reflected in the curricular structure and impel course revision.

• *Changes in educational technology:* As an example, the proliferation of microcomputers on college and university campuses has made it possible to use computer-aided learning in some curricular areas.

• *Changes in student interest:* Students vary from section to section of the same course, even in the same term, in their reasons for taking the course. The skilled learning manager adjusts, as much as possible, to these student interests by making minor revisions in the focus and presentation of the course material.

THE TEACHING ENVIRONMENT

No course is taught in isolation. The professor must be aware of the college and university's mission in society's educational system as well as of the social, political, and economic pressures on the college and university in the educational system. These factors interact to form the professor's environment. The professor must also be aware of the diversity of the student body. As with all managers, the professor as learning manager wears many hats and assumes many roles—both within the academic community and within society itself.

The Institutional Environment

The institution's mission is usually mandated by its founders, sponsors, or major funding agency. It is carried out by a Board of Trustees or a Board of Governors who set general policy. The board members' terms of office vary as do their methods of appointment. Most colleges and universities seek prominent persons interested in higher education to be on their governing board. The board usually has one or more faculty representatives. Board members also include alumni representatives and, increasingly, a member of the current student body.

All colleges and universities are accredited by various bodies to assure minimal standards of educational quality. Meeting these standards during periodic reviews by the accrediting bodies is a continuing concern of higher education. In addition, certain curricular programs have their quality regularly evaluated by a licensing body. These accrediting and licensing bodies influence curriculum and often influence support services as well.

There are major differences in environment between large and small schools and among public, independent, and religious schools. There are also environmental differences between residential-oriented colleges and commuter-oriented colleges, between daytime programs and evening schools. Some colleges and universities offer weekend programs for working professionals. These programs are usually intense and sharply focused. Summer-school programs offer a condensed curriculum, frequently in a more relaxed environment than the other academic terms.

As in all environments, there will be tensions, despite the fact that everyone desires the best possible education for the student body. There is frequently tension between professors (the faculty) and administration. College and university administrators are responsible for following established policy, attracting students, maintaining the physical plant, and providing a myriad of support services. Faculty is concerned with standards of scholarship and academic freedom. Pressures from the administration for credit-hour generation (i.e., high enrollment in a course) may conflict with faculty interests in interacting with students in small seminars. The professor wants to produce alumni who will be productive citizens as well as a credit to the college and to the professor's own teaching. Each faculty department wants to mount a program recognized for its high quality. The learning manager must operate effectively in this multifaceted institutional environment.

Social, Political, and Economic Environment

The educational needs of society change and interact with political and economic conditions. Change seems to come slowly in academia, especially in schools and departments with a large number of tenured faculty. Tenure is the career contract awarded the professor who successfully completes the probationary period established by the institution. The probationary period may not be more than seven years. The tenured faculty form the social establishment within which the professor must operate.

New programs to meet changing societal needs are developed by faculty-administration committees (sometimes with student input). These programs must first be approved by the faculty and administration. Final approval is by the Board of Trustees or Governors and, depending on institutional organization, by the state's Department of Higher Education. Funding of these new programs may come from various sources. Student tuition and fees generally account for only a portion of the costs of mounting an educational program. More often, funding comes from governmental sources, corporate giving, alumni fund drives, and endowments. Funding for high-technology programs involves expensive equipment which may become quickly outdated. High salaries for professors in these areas usually contrast with far lower salaries paid to professors in the humanities, where student interest is currently low. In this way, contemporary cultural values impinge on higher education. Schools may be more or less responsive to the needs of industry for a supply of graduates. In the current climate, many schools have special funding relationships with industry, especially in research institutes.

The college or university is asked to perform many roles in society. A land-grant school has obligations to the federal government, a state school to the state, a religious school to its sponsoring religion, etc. Some publicly funded two-year community colleges have an open-admissions policy and admit all community residents with a high-school diploma. These schools often devote a portion of their budget to remedial courses in English and in mathematics. The successful learning manager must be able to operate effectively in the social, economic, and political environment of the college or university where she works.

The Challenge of Student Diversity

Successful learning management takes into account the diversity of the student population. The approach to learning management is different in different schools and different among students at the same school. Demographic factors, personality factors, cognitive and motivational factors all contribute to student diversity and challenge the skills of the learning manager.

Demographic factors can be particularly challenging. Students of differing ages require different approaches to learning. Today, college campuses are apt to have a significant percentage of older (over 25 years of age) students. Learning management differs between single sex and co-ed schools. Ethnic differences bring an exciting variety of previous experiences and interests to the learning situation. Socio-economic differences bring different experiences and different external pressures on students. The majority of students today borrow money and/or work full or part-time to achieve a college degree. Geographic origin also brings differing experiences; some schools aim for a nationally distributed mix. The number of foreign nationals in the student body also adds demographic diversity to the college or university.

There is also student diversity in the cognitive area. This diversity includes differences in abilities, which are more or less reflected in tests of I.Q. and achievement. Homogeneity of abilities often occurs in schools with highly selective admissions policies. Schools that admit a broad range of students have more heterogeneity. In addition to diverse abilities, students also have diverse cognitive styles. Some students tend to generalize from their past perceptions, where other students individualize and sharpen differences among their past perceptions. There is also diversity in learning styles. Some students learn best by seeing, others by hearing, most by doing.

Personality variables clearly contribute to student diversity. Among these are differences in motivation, anxiety levels, tolerance of error, expectancy of success, and attention span. There are timid students and assertive students, students who talk in class and students who listen, students who seek out the professor and students who avoid bringing attention to themselves. Students have different levels of creativity. Some students have many new ideas each day and can relate one idea to another and come up with a completely new and original concept. Other students may have one new idea a week, and some students never seem to possess a new idea or an original thought.

9

Finally, diversity exists because students have different reasons for taking a particular course, not to mention different amounts of time and effort they are willing to devote to a particular course. Ideally, the learning manager will allow for student diversity, finding it part of the challenge of teaching.

The Professor's Many Roles

The professor has many roles as a member of an academic community, as a member of a subject discipline, and as a member of the community. This primer focuses on the professor's role as a teacher and learning manager. However, as a member of the academic community, the professor is expected to participate in many aspects of college and university governance. These often entail working with other faculty and with members of the administration on a variety of committees, task forces, etc.

The professor's role as a member of a subject discipline entails keeping up with new information and developments in the discipline. The professor active in her discipline is usually involved in research, often in collaboration with colleagues at other colleges and universities. Activities often focus on one or more professional societies where the professor may, in addition to presenting papers and participating in panel discussions, become involved as an officer, an active committee member, or the editor of one of the society's publications.

The professor often takes an active role in the community, providing expert advice to government and industry. The professor, at times, represents the college or university in various community activities.

However, the primary focus of the professor business is teaching. The importance of the professor's primary role of educator, managing learning in contemporary society, cannot be overstated. The college or university mission and the social, economic, and political environment in which the professor works all have their effect on the program of learning—the curriculum. The often highly philosophical curricular discussions about what subjects should be taught and how to teach them are clearly a major societal concern and an important part of the professor business.

Chapter 2

PERSPECTIVES ON TEACHING

Learning management involves decisions about what approaches are best suited to student learning and what the student should learn. The goal is to provide the student with sufficient guidance and direction to achieve the objectives of the course or program of study. Upon completion of his or her studies, the student should understand the subject well enough to deal with related problems by applying the information and knowledge gained. The student can then use this knowledge to develop more information and new knowledge.

HISTORICAL PERSPECTIVES

In times past, the higher wisdom and inner mysteries of a culture were revealed to only a select few initiates who learned their profession by rote and practice. Socrates taught by leading students through a logical argument. His method of asking a series of questions to force them to think for themselves and to be critical of every assertion is well known. Aristotle is usually credited with introducing the deductive method, which uses logical inference to reason from a generalization to a particular case or instance. Francis Bacon introduced the inductive method, i.e., reasoning from particular instances to a generalization or a verification of hypothesis. This inductive approach to learning is, essentially, what is now called the "scientific method."

Although a combination of the deductive and the inductive methods was the approach to knowledge used in the early 19th century, the lecture was the primary method used in classroom teaching. Students learned by rote memorization and presented recitations in class. Dickens made fun of this in *Hard Times:* "In this life, we want nothing but Facts, sir; nothing but Facts!" Mental discipline, which held that learning such subjects as Greek and Latin was "good for the mind," was a dominant notion. This notion was based on the assumption that mental discipline would help in learning other things. However, learning research has disproved this idea. At the end of the 19th century progressive education arose in reaction against mental discipline and the rote learning of facts.

The concepts involved in progressive education, which dominated educational approaches through the first part of the 20th century, are generally associated with John Dewey. Dewey believed that lectures fail when students are passive listeners and that students need to be actively involved in the learning process. The one concept most often associated with Dewey is "learn by doing." Students learned by being active, by participating in the learning process. Dewey conceived problem solving as the basic classroom method. The teacher's task was to arrange a problem situation for the students to solve.

The methods used in the past may be listed as follows:
- Rote learning
- Socratic method
- Deductive method
- Inductive method (scientific method)
- Learning by doing
- Problem solving.

All these methods are useful for learning some things at some times. Learning researchers who have evaluated these methods generally agree that learning meaningful information is superior to rote memorization of facts, and that active learning is superior to passive. Similarly, they have found that directed or guided learning is superior to unguided or incidental learning.

EDUCATIONAL IDEALS AND PURPOSES IN HIGHER EDUCATION

The subject expert may not be aware of how many philosophic values are intrinsic to education. Yet everyone, in all walks of life, has strong notions about what a student "ought" to know, what a student "ought" to learn, and what constitutes an educated person. While the student's job is to learn, what learning will best equip the student with the knowledge and skills to be a contributing member of society?

Clearly, the educated person must be able to do more than recite a list of memorized facts to contribute to society. Facts can be easily obtained when needed. Education involves the ability to approach a problem to obtain an optimal solution.

Ideals for education have varied throughout history. Educational philosophy in the Western world has roots going back to Plato's great dialogue "The Republic," in which he sets forth a program for education. To Plato, education occurred in the context of producing the ideal state. Plato had a world view and a view of what the human being is capable of learning. Advanced education required that the student understand such values as Truth, Justice, and the Good.

Rousseau, too, wanted to produce an ideal state and eliminate the corruption in the world. Rousseau felt that working from within the political system was hopeless; the changes necessary to eliminate corruption were too great. He believed that a whole new approach was needed, with small societies of people working together for the common good. In *Emile* he expressed his belief that all things which God created are good and that man has destroyed the natural goodness of God's creation. Therefore, students should learn from nature and be given the freedom to express their own inherent goodness.

John Dewey was concerned with educating for democracy. He believed that the ideal citizen should be able to ask the right questions and solve problems using the scientific method. Ideally, citizens should be able to reach consensus on societal issues.

Many other authors have written about the purpose of education for society in the 20th century. Alfred North Whitehead in *The Aims of Education* (p 102) states that:

> Education is discipline for the adventure of life; research is intellectual adventure; and the universities should be homes of adventure shared in common by young and old. For successful education there must always be a certain freshness in the knowledge dealt with. It must either be new in itself or it must be invested with some novelty of application to the new world or new times. Knowledge does not keep any better than fish. You may be dealing with knowledge of the old species, with some old truth; but somehow or other it must come to the students, as it were, just drawn out of the sea with the freshness of its immediate importance.

Everyone agrees, in the United States, that each individual is entitled to equality of educational opportunity. However, this does not mean that each individual has the same motivation or ability to take advantage of the opportunity offered, no matter how knowledge is presented. Berkson argues that education cannot be defined apart from the society in which that individual is to live. The values of the society are derived from the cultural heritage of the society (Berkson). Alan Bloom's book, *The Closing of the American Mind,* reached the bestseller list with questions about what information should be taught as part of the culture. He believes that old notions of the culture should be retained. Other authors argue that the experiences of various ethnic groups and of women were neglected in the old notions of American culture. In the late 1960s and early 1970s, students demanded "relevance" in the curriculum. In the late 1980s, many students seem to be career-directed in their choice of a curricular program. However, both employers and college professors increasingly recognize that the older, more rigorous educational goals for student reading, writing, and mathematical skills are also needed for contributing, productive citizenship.

Toward what cultural ideals should professors direct their students? This is a difficult philosophical question that most college and university professors are neither trained for nor have sufficient leisure to contemplate. Yet this question underlies many discussions about academic programs within institutions of higher education.

CURRENT CURRICULAR ISSUES

At Issue: A "Core" to the Liberal Arts? Many colleges which had reduced the number of required courses are reconsidering whether there is or should be a core group of courses which a college or university graduate should be expected to have studied. This question has recurred in higher education over the past hundred years. Criticism abounds that the student left to choose his or her own course of study takes scattered courses and never achieves a coherent curriculum or studies any subject in depth. Students who have chosen their own course may have followed a particular subject of interest and never gained any breadth of knowledge. Some colleges have re-established a core of required courses; others have re-established distribution requirements in arts and humanities, social and behavioral sciences, and natural and mathematical sciences. Some colleges offer interdisciplinary problem-oriented curricula. At issue is the question of what a core should be. Many complain that multi-ethnic, multi-cultural and women's studies on the one hand and global-cultural awareness studies on the other are neglected in traditional cores or in a Great Books approach to higher education.

At Issue: Multi-ethnic, Multi-cultural and Women's Studies: Studies of the development of the western industrialized world have dominated higher education in the United States. Many claim that this has resulted in exclusive emphasis on white male contributions. A response on many campuses has been the establishment of departments or programs such as Afro-American Studies and Women's Studies. Critics of this response believe that contributions of various ethnic and cultural groups and of women should be integrated into each and every course.

At Issue: Global Cultural Awareness: The emphasis on the western industrialized world in higher education has generated concern that American higher education has become parochial at a time when technologically and economically the world has become a global village. A global perspective in American higher education would offer courses and programs focusing on the art, literature, language, customs, history, etc. of Asia, Africa, South and Central America, and Australia, as well as on Western Studies. Students must prepare for life and work in a global village whose social, political, economic, and environmental concerns are interrelated. Students who can afford the cost should be encouraged to spend a year studying in a different country or culture. Other students should be encouraged to prepare to host visitors from other countries and to attain proficiency in at least one foreign language and its related culture.

At Issue: Inadequate High School Preparation: Some professors are finding that their students can't read, can't write, and have insufficient grounding in mathematics to do college work. International surveys show that the level of learning of students in the United States compares poorly with that of students from other industrialized countries. Colleges with open admission policies have had special problems. Professors who water down their offerings for poorly prepared students risk passing through the higher education system students who cannot satisfy entry-level employment requirements. Academia has responded to the problems of inadequate student preparation for college courses by establishing remedial programs, particularly in English writing, reading, and mathematics. These remedial programs include special pre-first-year summer sessions, tutoring programs, and academic skills centers. None of these remedial programs deal with deficiencies in general knowledge. Student deficiency in knowledge about science has been especially criticized. One response to this criticism has been the establishment of courses for non-majors that have a more general approach than courses for students intending to major in a particular branch of science. In the case of required non-credit remedial courses, for example, a student may not enroll in English composition until he or she has attained a certain level in remedial writing. However, the student may enroll in such courses as anthropology, political science, or history—all of which generally assume writing ability. This is a major problem.

At Issue: Ability to Write Standard English: The widespread use of objective tests in school systems and in college has led to a generation of students and alumni who have very little experience writing standard English. Students who possess proficient written communication skills are in great demand by employers for jobs at every level. Even individuals specializing in mathematically-oriented technical subjects must be able to communicate clearly to others in standard written English. Many colleges are reinstituting required first-year English composition courses. Many colleges are asking their faculty to emphasize writing in all course work, and some colleges have established a proficiency-in-writing test as a graduation requirement. Teaching writing skills in addition to course content becomes a time-consuming issue for the professor. In order to establish good writing skills, the student must have a great deal of experience with writing. Also, proficient writing develops with feedback. This means that the professor must add to evaluating the learning of course content the time-consuming tasks of evaluating student writing and having the student revise writing assignments until proficiency is attained.

At Issue: How Much and What Kind of Computer Education? Computer literacy was a buzz word in the 1970s and early 1980s. It referred to teaching all students the history of computers, how they work, and the fundamentals of a programming language. In retrospect, knowledge of the history of computers and how they work is not essential to learning how to use them. At issue is the value of learning how to program a computer. This knowledge is clearly useful, but not essential to operating computer applications such as word processing, spread sheets, and simple file processing systems. Students in various fields will have differing needs for computer education. All students will find that a knowledge of word processing will help them attain writing proficiency. Students in the arts may choose to learn graphic design applications. Students in business will learn file processing, spread sheet, and database applications. Social scientists may learn a statistical application. Natural and mathematical scientists, engineers, and others in technical areas will want to know computer architecture as well as programming languages.

At Issue: Liberal Arts vs. Job Training: The relevance and usefulness of courses and curricula for future occupations versus the relevance and usefulness of a broad, liberal arts education is a continual issue in higher education. There is a great deal of difference between a liberal arts program and a professional studies program in business, computer science, or the allied health professions. A professional program in law, medicine, and theology is a graduate program for students whose undergraduate preparation has been in a relevant liberal arts major. Liberal arts programs foster critical inquiry, logical analysis, problem solving, and creative ability. Students, and some employers, often fail to see that liberal arts programs provide skills relevant to a rapidly changing world. A professional studies program in business, computer science, or the allied health professions provides its graduates with the skills required for entry-level positions in these fields. However, further advancement generally requires a graduate degree. The more technical training provided by the professional studies programs may also be based on licensing requirements provided by the profession or by the state where the license is issued. The professor needs to be aware of the orientation and the expectancies of the particular program in which he teaches. Rapidly changing technology makes today's skills obsolete tomorrow. Therefore, the professor in a professional studies program is well advised to balance teaching the skills required for the job today with teaching the concepts and the modes of thinking required to keep the job tomorrow.

The wide variety of curricular programs and the numerous approaches to higher education are indicative of a pluralistic society. For the professor, the resultant diversity of students represents a major challenge to his learning management skills.

Chapter 3

ASPECTS OF LEARNING

To learn means to be able to do something that could not be done before. Psychologists refer to learning as a change in the behavior of the organism. This change in behavior applies to higher learning as well as to simple learning. Just how learning occurs in the brain is not yet known. Presumably, neural modification occurs, perhaps of synaptic connections in the central nervous system. Whatever the route, learning means change.

While professors are not expected to be experts in the psychology of learning, their teaching will improve by knowing some of the factors that influence learning and by understanding how these factors affect student learning. These include:

- Reward and punishment
- Problem-solving and insight
- Motivation and personality research
- Intelligence
- Cognitive science.

REWARD AND PUNISHMENT

Knowledge about the effects of reward and punishment comes from a psychological research area called "behaviorism." Behaviorism studies what organisms do. Its dominance in educational psychology accounts, at least in part, for the emphasis on performance measures associated with reinforcement theory. A significant body of laboratory research is available concerning reinforcement theory, i.e., learning "measured by the relative frequencies of speed of responses in the same situation" (Estes, p 320). Estes points out that these responses do not seem to apply in less-controlled circumstances.

The concept of reward, to the behavioral psychologist, refers to increasing the likelihood of repeating a behavior rather than to pleasure or satisfaction. On the one hand, the professor's recognition of the prepared student will increase the probability that the student will be prepared the next time. On the other hand, recognition of the unprepared student may have an unfortunate result. The concept of punishment, to the behavioral psychologist, is something that decreases the frequency of the immediate preceeding behavior, not something that makes the student angry or sad. Corrections of incorrect responses are intended to be punishing. Red marks on papers and grades, in some instances, may be punishing. Negative reinforcement increases the frequency of the behavior immediately preceding the response, especially when the reinforcement is stopped. For instance, a common example of negative reinforcement is the noise from a seatbelt buzzer which stops when the seatbelt is fastened. In academia, one example might be a student beginning to write a term paper about which he or she has been uptight and tense. The process of writing can actually remove the continuous negative tension stimulus.

Essentially, the behaviorist looks at the immediately preceding behavior and tries to reinforce it. The professor's problem is deciding what will be positively reinforcing or punishing for a particular student. One student may thrive on being corrected while another student may be embarrassed (punished) by praise. Effective use of behavioral techniques requires that the professor know the student(s) well.

In addition to reinforcement by rewards and punishment, behavioral psychologists have developed techniques of cueing, shaping, and modeling behaviors. Cueing, also called prompting, refers to arranging stimuli that will evoke a desired response. "Repeat-after-me" is a simple example. Following establishment of a desired response, the prompt is gradually withdrawn until it is no longer needed. Shaping refers to approximating a correct response and gradually rewarding only those responses which are more accurate or precise. For example, in improving student accents when learning a foreign language, any understandable response is initially rewarded. Gradually a better and better accent is shaped by rewarding successive improvements or approximations of the desired accent. In modeling, the correct response is demonstrated by the professor. The student is rewarded when his or her response corresponds to the professor's.

Behavioral psychology has provided the theoretical background and techniques for drill-and-practice learning. The field of behavioral psychology has influenced programmed instruction. Behaviorists emphasize active rather than passive learning. Reinforcement theory shows that occasional rather than continuous rewards lead to learning that is retained longer. In general, behavioral psychology has shown that punishment should be avoided as a means of influencing behavior because the response to punishment is unpredictable.

PROBLEM-SOLVING AND INSIGHT

While the behavioral psychologists studied learning at the stimulus-response level, gestalt psychologists examined the whole structure of the learning situation. They examined problem-solving mainly as part of perception and emphasized insight, organization, and form or, in modern parlance, models for learning.

Insight occurs after examining a problem situation in some context and suddenly "seeing" a relationship or some organization among various aspects of the situation. Often an incubation period for the problem is required before insight occurs. Frequently, when the problem is put on a mental "back burner," the solution to the problem suddenly comes to mind. This often occurs when thinking about something else or when working on another task. Waking up in the middle of the night with an insight is often reported.

Problem-solving is goal directed in its attempt to solve a particular problem or to reach "closure" in a particular situation. Closure refers to the tendency to mentally complete a pattern with only some clues, such as closing an open circle, or "seeing" that a tool is necessary to reach an objective. Problem-solving often involves organizing information into patterns as a way of simplifying observations. Once a particular pattern has been recognized and defined, the pattern becomes easier to find again. At the same time, the tendency to continue along a particular organized train of thought and not to see variations or to look for new solutions is common.

Findings from gestalt research show that learning with understanding is recognized, recalled, and retained much longer than rote learning. Rote learning, i.e., memorization, requires much practice. However, learning with understanding can happen in one step. A flash or an insight requiring no practice means that understanding the derivation and use of a formula in mathematics or understanding the mechanism of a chemical reaction is preferable to memorizing its formula. Such learning with understanding transfers more easily to new situations. "Mental set" or preparedness to learn is also important—it might be called the ability to focus on problem-solving.

For the professor, the findings from gestalt research mean that course material should be arranged so that its overall organization is clear to the class from the beginning. Subsequently, a more detailed level of organization can be presented. By the same token, such organization implies that step-by-step development of an argument must be placed in an organized pattern that the student can easily follow. Gestalt psychology would also state that "what-leads-to-what" should be laid out for students so that they can quickly grasp an organized pattern. Gestalt psychologists would define the professor's role as guiding and encouraging students to discover solutions to problems, confirming good solutions, and correcting weak ones.

MOTIVATION AND PERSONALITY RESEARCH

Learning can't happen unless the student is ready for the learning experience. A variety of psychological studies have emphasized the importance of the preparedness of the student for learning. These studies have focused on several factors:

- Maturation
- Motivation
- Arousal and attention
- Environment and culture
- Anxiety and fear
- Small group behavior.

Maturation is important for readiness, as in "reading readiness" at the elementary school level. At the college level, late adolescents differ greatly in their maturity and preparedness for the college experience. Indeed, for a given student, the type of learning experience offered by one college can be more beneficial than the type offered by another college. For instance, some colleges, often the smaller ones, offer more personal attention and faculty counseling to students than others. Some colleges have a more rigorous academic curriculum than others. These colleges require that the student have the maturity and the self-discipline to focus more on course work than on extra-curricular activities. Universities, which at times have large undergraduate classes of over 100 students, require that the student be sufficiently mature to take responsibility for his or her own learning. At best, these courses provide assistance by a graduate student to complement the professor's lectures.

Motivation is very important to learning. The perceived relevance of subject matter will have a great influence on the student's motivation to learn. Professors have found that older, more mature students returning to school for continuing education frequently have more motivation to learn than the average college-age student. Older, more mature students know why they want to attend college. The average college-age student often has less motivation and attends college because of parental expectations or because it is "the thing to do." Perceived relevance of subject matter as a motivational factor is related to occupational goals as well as to student maturity. Some courses are seen by students as more relevant to occupational goals than others. However, the student has a limited notion about what might be relevant. The student who takes courses only for their perceived relevance is narrowing future opportunities. Both the curricular program and the faculty can encourage students to take courses that will broaden their knowledge base beyond narrow occupational goals. Nevertheless, required courses may suffer from student perceptions of their limited relevance.

Motivation is an important factor with students who focus more on learning to be popular or on becoming a first-team athlete than on their studies. Such students, to their peril, may ignore early warnings of poor academic performance. For these students, spending time with friends or refining their athletic prowess or improving their leadership skills is not balanced with the academic requirements of the college experience. On the other hand, some students are driven only by the need to study for good grades. Such students also need to balance their focus with the more social aspects of the well-rounded college experience.

Arousal refers to the well-understood physiological state that is required for effective learning or action. Arousal contrasts with the "couch potato" stance. It relates to attention, focus, and preparedness for action. **Attention** fluctuates over time and in a classroom situation generally wanders every 20 minutes. Some research has suggested a 50-minute periodicity, though this may be student conditioning from previous high school experience. Attention has an environmental aspect. Today's students have grown up in an environment pervaded by radio and television, and many students have learned to mentally tune out advertisements and to focus their attention on both classroom assignments and radio or television at the same time.

Students, as well as many other members of society, may manipulate their arousal level with caffeine and over-the-counter drugs such as Nodoze. Such drugs do not improve attention. Eating tends to reduce arousal. This condition can be observed by any professor who teaches a class after lunch!

Environmental and cultural factors are known to strongly influence previous and present learning experiences and styles. These factors also influence the way a student thinks and feels. For instance, foreign students often have been trained in thinking patterns that reflect their culture. For the foreign student in any country, learning involves adapting thinking patterns to the environment and culture of the host country. Minority students frequently have difficulty adapting to the environment of those colleges in the United States that have been oriented to a white, male-dominated culture. These students are often extremely sensitive about their minority status. The women's movement, black consciousness, and Hispanic awareness are just three examples of groups with their own feelings and sensitivities that affect learning.

Likewise, the environment and culture of particular individuals, regardless of majority or minority status, affect the way they will learn. The same subject material may actually mean different things to different individuals. The diversity of student backgrounds clearly will influence the way the professor must manage classroom learning and will also affect the goals which the professor can set for the class. Although it is simpler to set goals and to design instruction for a homogeneous group of students, working with a heterogeneous group of students can frequently lead to more learning for all concerned, the professor included.

Anxiety and fear negatively affect the student's ability to learn. Anxiety is usually differentiated from fear in that fear is considered "real" and anxiety is not. However, the body's physiological response is the same to both. Freshman students normally have anticipatory anxiety about college and about performing well in a particular course. This anxiety is allayed by knowing what the professor expects and by early feedback, which reassures the student that the work can be done as expected. Students have different anxiety levels. They respond differently to different kinds of learning situations and even to encouragement. In some situations, high-anxiety learners do better without feedback, while low-anxiety learners do better with continuous feedback. Occasionally a student is paralyzed by anxiety. Such students should be referred to a counseling center.

Some students allay anxiety by taking tranquilizers and other drugs. While medicating against anxiety can have beneficial results on some occasions, students can overdo this method of combating anxiety.

Psychologists who study **small group behavior** have shown that students differ in both amount of learning and in satisfaction with learning depending upon the setting. When a small group begins to function as a single entity, members can learn from each other. The success of a group of four to six students depends on how well it operates as a single entity. Groups whose members resent being placed with others are rarely successful. Some students resent being placed with students of differing intelligence and motivation. They resent group members who will not cooperate or carry a fair share of the work assigned.

The professor considering small group behavior as a way to encourage learning should set clear goals for the group and articulate a structure for the work assigned. Small groups with unclear goals and work assignments usually do little. Groups establish their own norms and standards and tend to pressure members to conform. The skilled professor can take advantage of these characteristics to promote learning behavior in small groups.

While the motivational and personality factors involved in maturation, motivation, arousal and attention, environment and culture, anxiety and fear, and small group behavior are important to the psychology of learning, the overriding factor for learning is the interaction between students and professor. Experienced professors know that their interaction with a classroom group can differ from one section of a course to another, even in the same term. The interaction between professor and students in one class can be superb and in another, taught in exactly the same way, dismal. While the professor can try early in the term to adjust to the motivations and personalities of the student group, these adjustments don't always work. The professor can only hope that the students in the same course next term will interact positively to form a more cohesive group.

INTELLIGENCE

The concept of intelligence has changed over the years from a unitary one favored in the early 20th century to the contemporary multifaceted one. The unitary concept was supposed to reflect many abilities. Ability to perform academically was tested, to a greater or lesser extent, by the still pervasive IQ test, which provides a numerical indication of intelligence level. By the 1960s, Guilford had

already proposed a model of intelligence, which included opera-
tions, products, and contents (Guilford). In 1988, Sternberg presented
a triarchic model. This model differentiates internal mental processes, methods of dealing with the environment, and ways in which
the environment shapes intelligence (Sternberg, 1988).

The professor is thus faced with the challenge of tailoring presentation not only to level of intelligence, but to type of intelligence. It is
certainly germane to learning management to consider approaches
to learning that foster the kind of thinking that often leads to innova-
tion. At the same time, focused approaches to learning that foster
convergent, in-depth thinking about a subject area are also needed.

In the late 20th century, a student's numerical measure of intelligence is considered a product of both genetics and the environment.
The tests of aptitude (Scholastic Aptitude Tests) and achievement
(College Boards, MCAT, etc.) predict well how a student will do in
college, but predict poorly how successful a student will be later in
life—however "success" is measured.

COGNITIVE SCIENCE

Cognitive science, which may be traced to the 1950s, has emerged
at the end of the century as a highly important field impacting on
the psychology of learning (Gardner). Research in this field has been
very dependent on the computer for studies of thinking, memory,
and learning. Many of these studies base their findings on neuro-
science. One of the findings is the natural tendency for human beings to organize or classify events and knowledge. Another finding is
the redundancy of memory representations, which fluctuate ran-
domly in availability over time (Estes, p 331). In part because of the
computer model, teaching thinking skills involves a recognition, as
Sternberg (1987) points out, of three different components: executive
processes, the performance component, and the learning or knowledge component. Executive processes are meta components which
plan, monitor, and evaluate the individual's thinking. The performance component carries out thinking. The learning component
deals with learning how to think. These components are what the student acquires. Sternberg's concept of teaching thinking skills com-
plements the idea that specific facts or data can be easily retrieved
from outside sources, i.e., with the proliferation of computerized
databases, the student needs only to learn how to retrieve specific

facts or data from these sources. These concepts are one solution to coping with the information explosion which has generated too much information, even about a relatively circumscribed field, for anyone to retain in his or her head. Therefore, the student needs to learn how to find information and how to use it instead of internalizing the information itself.

One example of this line of computer-based research is the Soar system (Waldrop). Soar "reasons" in a goal-directed way; that is, it proceeds step by step. It keeps track in working memory of where it is in the solution process. Condition-action statements (if...then rules) are located in a storage location. The storage location is supposed to be analogous to human long-term memory. The storage location contains both factual information and how-to information. All rules are accessed simultaneously, i.e., in parallel. When no appropriate rule is found in storage, Soar begins to solve the subproblem of establishing an appropriate rule. The storage location "remembers" such solutions and thus is said to learn from experience. Of interest to professors and to all educators is the fact that Soar learns only when it is solving problems and that it speeds up with practice.

Systems such as Soar will be watched with great interest. No one believes that computers model even simple human thinking. Yet there is no question that some computer systems appear to do some things which human beings do—sometimes better. Whether or not the computer is an appropriate model for human cognition remains to be seen. Indeed, the entire analogy may prove to be misleading. The lesson for the professor is that the computer model for human thinking and learning may undergird a trend to differentiate being able to work with facts and knowing how to access (retrieve) them from having facts in one's head. Facts can be stored in many ways and readily accessed by those who know how. The student needs to learn the models and concepts that form the basis for the data and skills in each subject to be studied.

Part II

Learning Management

Chapter 4

COURSE PLANNING
AND DESIGN

The new professor is hired on the basis of subject expertise, often with only a few weeks lead time to teach several courses. This frequently happens when the professor is asked to teach existing courses in an established curriculum. That professor needs to know how to immediately implement a general course description with his own plan and course design. (Preparation of new courses is covered in Chapter 11: Developing as a Learning Manager.) Course planning and design includes the steps needed to accomplish the goals for learning, which the professor establishes for the course.

The specific steps involved in course planning include:

• Learning the organizational context and the environment in which the course will be taught;

• Specifying goals and objectives for the course and objectives for each class;

• Deciding the most effective sequence and methods of presenting course materials for learning;

• Planning activities and assignments to accomplish the goals and objectives set for learning;

• Designing methods of evaluating learning and means of grading student accomplishments;

• Summarizing the course objectives, topics to be covered, assignments and requirements in a written course syllabus.

THE INSTITUTIONAL CONTEXT

A course is planned in the context of a particular academic department and in the environment of a particular college or university. As discussed in Chapter 1, each college or university has a particular mission. For instance, some colleges and universities are private and associated with a particular religious group; others are public and supported by state, county, or local taxes. In a public college or university, a focus on religion would be strictly prohibited as a violation of the separation of the church and state.

Some colleges are small with classes of 20 students or less. The university, especially at the undergraduate level, is often characterized by large classes of more than 100 students. Courses must be planned and designed very differently for a large class than for a small one. Students in small classes can interact easily with the professor and course design can be more individualized and flexible. Large classes are often characterized by a formal lecture period which is followed by smaller laboratory or discussion groups led by a teaching assistant, usually a graduate student in the department.

The goals of a faculty teaching a particular subject in one college or university may differ from the goals of a faculty in a different place teaching the same subject. Course planning and design in a college focusing on the theoretical aspects of a subject field will be very different from the course planning in a college focusing on the practical, skill-related aspects of the same subject. The new professor must quickly learn the mission and the goals of the particular faculty in which he plans to teach. This will provide direction for planning a course designed to teach theoretical concepts or job-related skills. This subject context is usually defined during the candidate's job interview.

Some background on the students themselves is also essential. Course design for first-year students is very different from course design for upper-classmen who have already learned to work with less structure than they had in high school. Upper-classmen are more self-motivated and goal directed, especially when taking courses in their major field. First-year students usually need detailed assignments and often benefit from more frequent testing to monitor their learning. Upper-classmen often work more independently on larger projects, especially if they plan to attend graduate school. Some students, especially in the two-year colleges, may require remedial assistance with their writing and mathematics. In more selective colleges and universities, course design can assume a higher level of student ability to write and/or to cope with mathematical concepts. A pre-test during the first course session can be used to define the general level of student knowledge in the class. The level of teaching can then be adjusted to complement the level of the students' background in the subject field.

In many colleges and universities today, older students are enriching the classroom once characterized by students in their late teens and early twenties. After World War II, the returning veterans enriched college and university classrooms. Today many students are returning to school after years of work experience; added to these students are retirees, displaced homemakers, and "empty nesters." Most professors have found that this mix of age and maturity levels benefits everyone involved in the learning process.

In addition to the age, intellectual, and maturity levels of the student, the professor must also become aware of the activities and responsibilities which students undertake in addition to their class schedules. These can include part-time or full-time employment, family responsibilities, and involvement in campus activities. Many either add stress or cause stress, which can impede student learning. The professor, aware of these activities and responsibilities and sensitive to their demands, can often minimize this stress with a little flexibility in scheduling requirements. Students will usually work doubly hard for the professor who helps them to balance their outside responsibilities with the requirements for the course. This is an argument for sensitivity and awareness, not weak content; it is an argument for flexibility, not lax standards. Generally after the first semester or year of teaching, the professor will revise course designs to adjust to the needs of students. This fine-tuning is a reflection of the professor's teaching expertise and experience.

GOALS AND OBJECTIVES

Goals and objectives are determined for a given course in a specific institutional setting in order to specify what learning the student should have achieved at the end of the course. Society expects that students who have completed a certain course will have certain skills and knowledge. The institution may have established learning expectancies for writing or computer use that apply to a given course. Lower level courses within the curriculum are expected to provide the foundation for higher level ones. The professor knows what he expects students to accomplish within a particular course. Appropriate goals for all courses include teaching reasoning, thinking, and professional values. Finally, but clearly not least important, students enroll in a course with their own expectancies about what they will learn.

Teaching reasoning would appear to be a suitable goal for any course in higher education. Nisbett et al. present results to show that students can be taught how to reason; they conclude, "Now that there are some clues about the nature of the rules that people actually use and can be taught, we may be able to proceed more efficiently to identify the ones that are most useful and how they can best be taught." Some of the methods of classroom presentation suggested in Chapter 5 as well as the suggestions in subsequent chapters for laboratory study and outside assignments can be used for teaching reasoning.

Teaching critical thinking requires awareness of the laws, models, theories, and methods of analysis in the subject. The student also needs to be taught the style of thinking that is characteristic of the discipline. Research does not yet show how to teach critical thinking at the college level. Pintrich, in a brief review, indicates that while there is wide interest in teaching critical thinking in higher education, the results are not directly applicable in the classroom, and it may be that there are subject matter differences. Currently, cognitive psychologists are studying how thinking works; they believe it involves organization and making connections of new material with old material. Organization and making connections both depend on what the student starts with. The organization is facilitated by knowing how the subject is organized—what the glue is which holds the facts together. This is reflected in the methods of categorization and validation, schools of thought, and styles of each subject. Some fields emphasize analysis, others emphasize synthesis; some comparison, others trends. Some appeal to authority, rigor of proof, or aesthetic taste in a given period and environment. It is helpful for the professor to consider how he makes judgments. Pintrich indicates that it is helpful for the professor to model and verbalize his own strategies for critical thinking (p 81).

Values need to be considered for all fields, especially today when ethical values are the focus of so much attention. A value might be information that is worth learning or a way of thinking that is useful. Brown and Atkins point out that "many physicists value quantitative measurements, pure mathematicians are concerned with rigour of proofs, and historians with the quality of different types of evidence" (p 56).

There is increasing concern with teaching students about values. Collins puts it eloquently:

> While we know their answers cannot in the end be discovered, we who teach must nonetheless ask our students (as we must ourselves) to take such questions ... seriously so that when they are faced, as they inevitably are, with the necessity of making a choice, of deciding what is worth dying for, lying for, going to prison for, they will have some examined vision of what they believe to be good, some earned grounds upon which to make, with both humility and conviction, as wise a judgment as they can. (p 29)

Collins suggests that "one way to teach students to make difficult moral judgments, one way to help them toward some answers to the truly important human questions is to teach them to interpret, carefully and honestly, whatever texts or data the discipline deals with, to come to considered judgments upon them" (p 27). The significant points about presenting values in the classroom seem to be:

- Recognizing that each subject has implicit values;
- Determining which values to present implicitly and explicitly;
- Including value considerations in the presentation.

Values may be presented implicitly by the professor's stance and attitude as well as by the level, type, and quality of work required in the course. Values are presented explicitly by consideration of certain value or moral issues using some lecture, discussion, or combination method. Issues may also be incorporated into assignments and individual laboratory work.

The actual goals and objectives defined for a course are linked to the informational content in the course, the competencies to be achieved by taking the course, and the values (specified and implied) to be communicated by the professor. Information content is the subject matter of the course; it defines the cognitive knowledge that the student is expected to gain. Competencies refer to the skill(s) that the student will acquire as a result of taking the course. For example, a student who has completed a course in advanced conversational Spanish would be expected to converse in Spanish. Similarly, a student who has completed a course in FORTRAN would be expected to write a computer program in that language.

Some educators go further and differentiate between goals, objectives, and performance objectives in terms of their levels of specificity. Performance or behavioral objectives are the most specific level. Performance objectives refer to competence or skill as a result of having taken a course. They are specifically measurable. According to Mayer, performance objectives include the performance, the condition under which it will be measured, and the criterion (e.g., speed, accuracy, quality) that will be used in the measurement. Performance objectives are basic to mastery learning and personalized systems of instruction. They do not include a description of the content and procedures that will be used in teaching or the experiences that the student will have during a course. They refer only to outcomes. The difference, according to Mayer, is similar to that between the process of baking and the final product (outcome) of bread (Mayer, p 32).

Those educators in favor of performance objectives argue that students need to know what they are supposed to do and that the only way to determine what students have learned is to test the results of learning in a specific reproducible way. Those against the use of performance objectives argue that there is a great deal of learning that occurs as a result of instruction and study that cannot be conveniently measured. As pointed out by Eble, to limit 1earning to what can be objectively tested reduces learning to what is testable (p 451).

Many value-related goals are difficult to specify as performance objectives. Certainly values are difficult to test for. The professor may decide to assess values indirectly. Often the professor will not want to include a value-related goal on a syllabus or to specify such a goal to students. Nevertheless, for planning purposes the learning manager will want to consider what values should be part of the course design. The professor may also wish to share his own value system with the class as a way of helping the students to understand a particular point of view. In an economics class, for instance, the professor who is a Keynesian economist would have an entirely different point of view from the Marxist. Students should also be instructed that they are not expected to adopt the professor's value system but to understand his orientation. However, the student is expected to internalize values related to goals, such as the merit of critically assessing evidence for decision-making.

Various attempts have been made to establish hierarchies of educational objectives for higher education. The most famous attempt was compiled by the Committee of College and University Examiners chaired by Benjamin Bloom: *Taxonomy of Educational Objectives: The Classification of Educational Goals,* commonly known as Bloom's Taxonomy. The taxonomy provides the best thinking from Bloom's committee about different levels of cognitive and affective (values) learning. The cognitive taxonomy places knowledge that requires recall at the lowest level of learning. The next higher level of learning is comprehension; however, comprehension is the lowest level of understanding. The application level requires the use of abstractions in particular and concrete situations. Objectives at the analysis level involve a breakdown of elements, relationships, or organizational principles. Objectives at the synthesis level involve putting parts or elements together to form a whole. At the highest level, evaluation requires judgments about the value of material or methods for given purposes. The five levels of the affective domain are: (1) receiving (being sensitized to); (2) responding; (3) valuing; (4) conceptualizing a value or organizing a value system; and (5) internalizing a value or value system. Bloom's hierarchy is helpful in considering goals and objectives. (See Appendix A for an outline).

Defining course goals and objectives helps to focus the information content, competencies, and values which the student should derive from a course. The professor must select the most important aspects of the subject from a potentially overwhelming amount of information and show how these aspects relate to things the student already knows. Learning requires associating and relating current knowledge to new information. To gain new information, the student must also learn how to learn in a particular field. Because there is so much information in any field and because the student needs to know how to locate, use, and evaluate the information, *learning how to learn* is an important goal. The general competency goal for any course can be determined by expectations common to professionals in the field. General value-related goals might include the ability to think creatively and critically and to understand the significance of knowledge in the field.

Most goals and objectives need not be specified or even recorded, though they are needed for course planning and design. However, some goals and objectives should be included in the course syllabus. These would include the information or the competencies the student should gain from the course. These goals and objectives provide a structure for learning and describe how the learning will be evaluated. The student should be clear about what he or she has to accomplish to do well in the course.

The professor's problem in determining content objectives usually arises from the large quantity of material that needs to be sifted and evaluated for presentation. Suggestions for content may be obtained from: (1) syllabi from previous instructors (when available); (2) standard texts; (3) course descriptions for related higher level courses in the curriculum; (4) previous and lower level courses in the curriculum, and; (5) any other standard curricula.

To determine specific course objectives, the professor must ask himself what the course is designed to accomplish in the context of a departmental program or curricular track. How, specifically, will the student's knowledge be increased as a result of taking the course? What are the new ideas that the student can apply to solve appropriate problems? What new tasks can the student accomplish that he or she did not know how to accomplish before taking the course? What new skills can the student employ that he or she did not have before taking the course? The answers to these questions can usually assist in defining course objectives.

In defining course objectives, the following factors should also be considered:

• The prerequisites for the course—what the student is expected to know before taking this course;

• The preparedness of the students taking the course—prior education and maturity must be considered;

• The concreteness or the abstractness (or any combination thereof) of the course material—this factor must be considered in combination with the previous two factors;

• The length of the course—the objectives must be able to be achieved by the average student within the time limits of the course;

• The expectations of future professors or employers for persons who have successfully completed the course—the specific ideas, tasks, and/or skills the student can be expected to have learned.

Once the professor has his goals and objectives clearly defined for the course, the subject content (and often the methods required to present the content to the students) usually becomes clear. Some colleges and universities now require faculty to post course outlines with objectives for students to read before registering to take the course.

Specifying course goals and objectives for the course as a whole can be considered as specifying at a macro level. Specifying objectives for each class session can be considered as specifying at a micro level. Yet specifying objectives at the class session level can assist both professor and student in maintaining a consistent focus to learning management and to learning.

SEQUENCE OF PRESENTATION

After the goals and objectives for the course have been defined, the next step in course planning and design is to determine the sequence for presenting course content. Generally, this sequence consists of units presenting specific aspects of the course. These units are usually labelled and often listed week by week or even class by class. For the student, this sequence represents the flow of the course and an indication of when quizzes, tests, and exams will be given and/or when term papers or projects will be due. A skeletal course schedule (omitting defined units of study), which might be used for a quarter-based course or for a semester-based course, is given below:

QUARTER SCHEDULE	**SEMESTER SCHEDULE**
(12-week term)	(16-week term)

1. Introduction	1. Introduction
2.	2.
3.	3.
4.	4.
5. Review	5.
6. Midterm exam	6.
7.	7. Review
8.	8. Midterm Exam
9.	9.
10. Term Projects Due	10.
11. Review	11.
12. Final Exam	12.
	13.
	14. Term Papers Due
	15. Review
	16. Final Exam

These schedules may need to be modified to allow for the following options:

• Giving several tests instead of mid-term and final exams;

• Omitting the review as a separate class period;

• Omitting a classroom session to allow students to work independently on a paper or project;

• Providing for a field trip to a relevant off-campus location.

These are only some options that might be considered to modify the skeletal course schedule. There may be many opportunities for assessment and no formal examinations per se. In cumulative courses such as introductory language courses, review may occur at each session. The creative professor will think of other options which will contribute to student learning of the course content.

In planning the course schedule, the professor must keep holidays in mind, especially in schools where students must travel a distance to return home. The school calendar will indicate school holidays. Scheduling a test or exam for the class immediately preceding or following a holiday is unwise. Absenteeism is frequently high the day before a holiday, and students are seldom prepared to take tests and exams scheduled for the class immediately following a holiday.

Many colleges and universities schedule a student evaluation of teaching for one of the class periods toward the end of the term. The time required for students to complete the evaluation form will vary and should be considered in planning this class session.

METHODS FOR PRESENTING COURSE CONTENT

Specific options for actually presenting the course materials are discussed in Chapter 5: Classroom Presentation; Chapter 6: Laboratory Learning; and in Chapter 7: Course Assignments. In general, once goals and objectives have been established and the sequence of course content has been outlined, the methods of reaching them are often constrained by factors which the professor cannot control. These may include class size, available equipment, inadequate facilities, and limited support services. For instance, in a class of 250 students, discussion is almost impossible and a laboratory period would strain the physical facilities and support services of most colleges and many universities.

In reviewing the literature about the effectiveness of different methods of teaching, Brown and Atkins conclude that lectures are "at least as effective as other methods of presenting information and providing explanations" (p 11). Lectures can be used to generate interest in the subject (p 19). Discussion and seminar classes are "usually better than other methods at promoting intellectual skills including problem-solving, and at changing attitudes, and about as effective as other methods at presenting information" (p 52). "Practical skills are obviously taught more effectively in laboratories" (p 9). Laboratories are also used to "improve understanding of methods of scientific enquiry" (p 9), to develop problem-solving skills, and for "nurturing professional attitudes." Values are generally taught by setting standards and by one's own attitude in presenting material. Since both standards and attitudes reflect values, specific discussion of values need not necessarily be part of the presentation.

ACTIVITIES AND ASSIGNMENTS

Within the general course schedule, the professor must plan how to present course content and also plan the activities and assignments, in and out of the classroom, which will enhance and reinforce the course content. The kind of activity chosen to enhance student learning is limited only by the skill and imagination of the professor. In-class activities, out-of-class assignments, and methods of presentation overlap. They are an important part of learning management.

EVALUATION

To assess the progress each student is making in learning the course content, the professor must design methods to evaluate learning during and after each unit of study as well as, more comprehensively, at the end of the course. Quizzes, tests, and exams have been traditional methods of evaluating student learning. However, there are many kinds of quizzes, tests, and exams—each with advantages and disadvantages. These are discussed in Chapter 10: Evaluation.

Methods other than the traditional ones may be just as effective or even more effective in evaluating student learning. Students can make presentations to the class describing what they have learned; such practice in oral discourse is valuable in itself. They can present projects completed outside of class which display skill in accomplishing a particular task, such as a work of art which demonstrates the command of a particular artistic medium or technique. A wealth of evaluative methods exist, and the creative professor can always devise new and unusual ones.

From the beginning of the course, though, the student must know how he or she is to be evaluated. Once the course has begun, the rules for evaluation should rarely be modified unless circumstances mandate that such a modification is the only effective way to evaluate student learning. Even then, many professors will seek student concurrence with the modification that has to be made.

The evaluative method(s) selected to assess student learning should reflect the goals and objectives of the course and complement the course design. Otherwise, the evaluative method is not accurately assessing the result of the learning process.

THE SYLLABUS

The course syllabus can be many things. The syllabus can include some or all of the following information:

- A statement of course goals and objectives for the course;
- An outline of course content and units of study;
- The prerequisite courses or knowledge or skill required for enrollment in the course;
- A list of requirements which must be completed to pass the course, including expectations about student attendance in class;
- The methods of evaluation of student effort and the percentage to be allocated to various course assignments, tests/exams, and projects/papers;
- A schedule of class meetings and dates when tests will be given and when papers and/or projects are due;
- A notice about when and where the professor will be available for consultation with students outside of class;
- A list of textbooks and other materials which the student must acquire for the course;
- A list of readings which the student is expected to sample or complete for the course;
- Other information which the professor deems valuable for the student to have at the beginning of the course.

The syllabus serves as a broad course guide for the student. In some colleges and universities, the course content and requirements parts of the syllabus may be used by the administration for student counseling and course selection. Customs and requirements about the form and content of course syllabi vary from one college or university to another. The new professor should ascertain the local customs as soon as possible. Sometimes, the new professor is given the syllabus of the former professor whose course the new professor is expected to teach. In this case, the syllabus serves as a guide for the professor. Also, the syllabus of a professor who is responsible for the content and learning outcome(s) of a particular course may be given to faculty teaching other sections of the same course. In this case, the syllabus serves not only as a guide to the professor, but also insures some commonality in learning outcomes when a course serves as a prerequisite to higher level ones in a particular course sequence. Otherwise, much time can be spent at the beginning of a course to bring all students to the same level of learning, unfortunately wasting the time of and boring the students who have already reached the level of learning expected for students taking the course. A syllabus checklist is included as Appendix B.

The syllabus should be distinguished from a set of course notes which the professor might wish to provide to assist student learning. Both individually developed syllabi and detailed course notes are the professor's intellectual property.

Chapter **5**

CLASSROOM PRESENTATION

This chapter focuses on classroom presentation of course content as a means of managing learning. Various methods of presenting course content are described, giving advantages and disadvantages for each method. This format is designed to assist the professor in planning the course and in determining methods which fit the subject matter and with which the professor will be comfortable. The chapter also discusses learning media and technology.

THE FIRST SESSION OF THE COURSE

The first session of any course is crucial for it often determines student attitudes for the rest of the course. The most skillful professors attest to the intellectual and emotional effort that goes into this first class session. Yet, no formula works each time, even for the most experienced and popular professors. The success of the course depends on the interaction between the teacher and the students in the class—a mix of personalities that changes every time the course is given. Communicating with this mix of personalities provides constant change and continual challenge, both of which contribute to the excitement and the fun of teaching.

How

Arrive early, bringing back-up chalk or markers for writing on the board. Check for erasers and any equipment that will be needed for the class. *Note:* Plan ahead and special order any audio-visual equipment or materials needed for this and for future sessions. Check with the department chairman or dean about specific procedures.

The professor will help early arrivals and latecomers to be sure they are in the correct classroom by writing her name on the board along with the course number, section, and course title.

The materials to be presented should be arranged in the order in which they will be used, placing a supply of syllabi near the door to minimize disruption by latecomers.

Begin on time, establishing an expectation of punctuality from the students. The professor usually introduces herself, specifying any preferred form of address and indicating any special qualifications she might have for teaching the course. The administrative tasks can be completed quickly by taking the roll, passing out materials, and explaining the syllabus. Any special assignments should be indicated and any student questions about the course should be answered. Latecomers will have picked up the extra syllabi placed near the door and will generally check after class to be certain they are on the class list (roster). After completing the necessary administrative chores as quickly as possible, the professor should use the first session to stimulate interest in the course content and to get right into it. The session should take the entire class period.

Present an introductory lesson, actively involving students as much as possible. This lesson should be well planned to create excitement for the classes to come and to generate interest in the subject matter. Don't worry about learning student names in this first session. Do concentrate on involving the class in the course content.

Methods for Learning Students' Names

Every student wants the professor to know his or her name as soon as possible. However, no rule says that the professor must know everyone's name by the second class session. In fact, one school of thought suggests that the professor can be more objective by not learning student names at all and by grading student learning only by evaluating tests, papers, and projects handed in. This school of thought is more persuasive for very large classes than for smaller ones.

The following methods for learning names are frequently used:
- Establishing a seating chart.
- Making name cards (folding 5"x 8" cards as a tent).
- Having students introduce themselves (professor takes notes).
- Having students complete a questionnaire about their background, their reasons for taking the course and what they hope to learn from it.
- Having students pair off and introduce each other.
- Taking photographs to put with name cards or questionnaires.

- Taking roll every session or having a sign-in sheet.
- Focusing on student names when returning assignments.

The professor who learns about the student as a person can often relate the course content to specific student interests. In addition, having students learn each other's names may help them to form working relationships important for the learning that is to be done. *Note:* Most colleges and universities do not establish a final class list (roster) until the second week of a term. The professor needs to determine the school's policy for students adding or dropping the course, and for withdrawing from it the second week or later in the term.

METHODS OF PRESENTING COURSE CONTENT

The most important factor in determining how to present material is the professor's own comfort with a method. The method may be great, the professor may believe it would achieve her goals and objectives, but if the method is not easily managed, it is best avoided.

Class size and institutional facilities (the availability of supplemental materials and equipment, preparation time for making slides, tapes, etc.) may also influence the choice of teaching method. Costs and budgets for supplemental materials and for class and student computer time must also be considered. In every case, the teaching method chosen should be the most effective means of communicating the subject matter. For example, art history requires effective visual illustration for which no amount of straight oral lecture can compensate.

Most professors will use a variety of methods during the course and often within the same session unless the size of the class is very large or very small. The very small class is often a seminar and the very large class is usually a lecture. Some combination of lecture and discussion is the most common classroom presentation method. In "The Rhythm of the Semester," Nash writes: "As in a musical composition, an instructor should try for variations of pace and mood throughout the semester, and most importantly, a proportionality in the presentation of material, a comprehensible arrangement of the notes." There must be both thematic continuity and attention to pacing and variation across the semester and within individual classes. In the end, Nash suggests "the teacher can shape the semester into a well-articulated organic form." In more prosaic terms, the overall structure of the semester will be outlined on the syllabus, including the goals for the student and the topics to be covered during each session.

Each session commonly begins with an introduction to the topic of the day or with an overview of the material to be presented. This introduction or overview should include a review of the previous session, linking the topic of the day to prior topics presented. A little humor is always welcome, as long as it is neither forced nor inappropriate. The major portion of the class session is devoted to the presentation of content material. A brief summary of this material at the end of the class is often useful to the students. Also, assignments to be worked on outside of class are usually made at the end of the class period. This format for the class session follows the familiar warm-up, review, presentation, and recapitulation typical of many course formats. The learning manager must be alert for student feedback indicating the need for a change of pace or for more illustration or explanation of the session content. At the same time, the professor must be alert to what Nash calls an example of "Classroom heart failure...ten weeks on the first book in an oversized reading list."

1. THE LECTURE

The lecture is the most common teaching method in higher education, perhaps because most professors were taught by this method and feel comfortable with it. Ericksen points out that "A well-organized lecture is an efficient means for presenting factual information, formal theories, and establishing patterns of knowledge, and for enhancing the motivation to learn" (Ericksen p 64). The points emphasized in his book include: (1) that remembering follows understanding (pp 53-68); (2) in guiding students to comprehend concepts, it is helpful to remember findings from cognitive psychology indicating that comprehension is based on deriving rules, principles, generalizations, themes, or ideas (pp 69-82, esp p 75); and (3) that it is possible to generate enthusiasm to learn (pp 41-53). These points are helpful in planning lectures.

How

Most students, though, will absorb only part of the information conveyed in a lecture. The experienced professor devises ways to reinforce the main points in her lecture, often with audio-visual materials borrowed from the media center or homemade. The one-hour lecture should include no more than a few major points, which are developed or argued and illustrated with examples. The method has three steps:

1) Present the points to be made.

2) Amplify and expand each point by presenting the subject matter the student is to learn.

3) Summarize the basic information presented.

The teacher may lecture from keywords and references, from brief or complete notes, or from full text. The impact of eye contact with students that comes from lecturing from keywords and references should not be underestimated. Students often follow the points to be made more easily if the teacher writes them on the blackboard or on a slide for an overhead projector.

The first-time teacher will learn in a few classes just how much material can be presented in each lecture and can expand or reduce the material presented accordingly. The student cannot process orally presented lecture material as rapidly as visually presented materials. Furthermore, the student is not controlling the rate of presentation. This rate may not be compatible with the student's learning style and needs.

A good lecturer combines presentation of subject material with elements of acting and preaching. The lecturer tells a story, being aware of voice, stress, emphasis, pacing of material presented, physical motion, and eye contact. The lecturer attempts to involve and relate to every student in the class.

Visual aids are helpful. The simplest is the traditional blackboard or whiteboard. Students absorb more information when they can add their own notes to a written handout or text instead of copying what a teacher writes on the board. Examples that a student can visualize will aid learning. The idea is to use the visual sense to support the auditory.

Advantages

- The teacher knows what was covered.
- Students are provided a common core of information.
- The teacher can present an attitude toward the subject and motivate student learning.
- Unfamiliar words and terms can be introduced, defined, and correctly pronounced.
- The material can be used again with possible revisions.
- The lectures can become the basis for a book.

Disadvantages

• The lecture is an easy *teaching* method, but a far less effective *learning* method.

• In general, according to psychological research, 80% of lecture information is not recalled by students one day later, and 80% of the remainder fades in a month.

• The average teacher does not have time to do the rehearsing required of a good lecturer, much less a superb one.

• The teacher is insulated from student feedback until test or exam time. When test results are disappointing, the teacher has only a few, time-consuming options for remedial work.

Recommendations

Lectures can and should be used with an understanding of their advantages, but they should be viewed as just part of the learning experience. The major amount of course-related information will be learned outside of the lecture. The students should be reading a text or other supplementary materials. Discussion periods may be added to the class. Laboratory work or studio experience may be required. Students may write course-related papers, work on a project, become involved in field work, etc.

2. INVITED SPEAKERS

Invited speakers add variety to the course, give the class the advantage of another specialist in the subject, and provide the opportunity for the students to gain an additional perspective on the subject. Speakers should be used, when the need arises, to extend and enhance the topics covered in the course. When famous scholars visit the school, a seminar is usually arranged to which interested faculty and students are invited.

How

Invite academic or professional colleagues who are willing and able to contribute to the course. Especially invite colleagues from other countries. Help these colleagues prepare to speak by explaining the general topic they should address. Provide them with the level of the students in the class and tell them what has already been covered in the course. The dean or department chairman may wish to be advised of an invited speaker, especially when the speaker is a well-known scholar. At times, other faculty or students could also be invited to attend this class. Inquire in advance about the possibility of an honorarium (usually not available) and make this clear to the speaker before he or she arrives—some colleagues may not speak without one. Also inquire about a budget for entertainment; a luncheon, dinner, or reception might be arranged.

Advantages
- Adds variety and a different perspective to the course.
- Provides a different role model and approach.
- Gives students an opportunity to meet another expert.

Disadvantages
- Allows someone else to control subject coverage.
- May contribute excessive or tangential details beyond scope of course.
- May bore the class or waste class time if speaker does not perform as anticipated.

Recommendations
Invited speakers can be used to advantage when they contribute to the goals and objectives of the course. Avoid having more than one class session with an outside speaker unless outside speakers are part of the course design. Take advantage of opportunities to invite visiting dignitaries to speak to specially arranged seminars.

3. DISCUSSION
Successful discussions are focused, informed, and conducted in many ways. The discussants must know what they are supposed to be talking about and have enough information to interact intelligently. However, "it is well to allow room [in discussions] for the unexpected. Sometimes the discussion takes off after the first question, and then the class develops its own direction and may develop ideas quite new to the instructor" (Scott p 142). The literature on discussion methods shows that discussion "is usually better than other methods at promoting intellectual skills including problem-solving, and at changing attitudes, and about as effective as other methods at presenting information" (Brown and Atkins, p 52). Brown and Atkins conclude that appropriate goals for discussion groups include: (1) developing communication; (2) attaining intellectual and professional competencies; (3) personal growth of students; and (4) teaching values (pp 56-57).

How
Pose a well-formulated problem or question in writing. Be sure the

problem or question is clearly stated and related to the purposes to be achieved. Writing the discussion question helps to insure clarity and enables all discussants to have the question, phrased in exactly the same way, in front of them during the discussion. Set a specific time limit for discussion or be prepared to step in when the discussion becomes bogged down. Terminate the discussion at a high level of interaction and involvement. In part, the purpose of discussion is to have the students continue arguing among themselves and with others after class. Another purpose is to have the students, on their own volition, consult authoritative sources to support their positions.

In formulating questions for discussion, the five aspects of questions discussed by Brown and Atkins might be considered (Brown and Atkins pp 69-72):

1) This aspect addresses conceptual, empirical and value-laden questions plus the necessity of deciding which kind of question will advance the discussion.

2) In the narrow-broad aspect, narrow questions result in short answers that bog down the discussion and broad questions may be bewildering.

3) The recall-thought aspect distinguishes between questions which assess knowledge and questions which require critical thinking.

4) The confused-clear aspect emphasizes that "clear questions are usually brief, direct, and firmly anchored in context" (p 71).

5) The encouraging-threatening aspect refers to the professor's style and its effect on encouraging or inhibiting student responses.

All of this means that productive, goal-oriented discussions require careful planning and skillful guidance.

Advantages

- Assesses student grasp and facility with the subject.
- Actively involves students.
- Appeals to many students.
- Interesting for the professor.
- Requires less preparation than lecture.
- Enables students to express feelings and opinions.
- Teaches interaction and tolerance for others' views.
- Encourages students to think.
- Provides opportunity for students to practice talking like a professional.
- Enables sufficient time to be spent on topics so they are mentally absorbed.

• Provides useful training for future efforts in job and community-related meetings.

• Provides the professor with a greater understanding of the students' personalities.

Disadvantages

• Students need a depth of experience or learning for truly informed discussion.

• Keeping track of how the topic was covered is difficult.

• Method is overused.

• Students often complain that "I paid to hear the professor, not other students."

• Method is not suitable for large classes.

• Students may hear and learn incorrect information.

• Student opinions may not only be uninformed, but also irrelevant to the discussion problem or question.

• Less subject material can be covered than in lecture.

Recommendations

Discussion should be used often. Use discussion to teach problem solving, develop critical thinking, promote the ability to make value judgments, and practice oral communication skills.

4. SMALL GROUPS

Small groups provide an opportunity for information sharing and problem solving with maximal individual participation. Small group theorists believe that a good group can attain more than the sum of the contributions of its individual members. These beliefs are based on the large body of research information that has been developing in this area since the 1940s.

A small group should have a maximum of 20 members. Groups with an odd number of members should be used for decision making, and groups with an even number of members should be used for consensus building. A group will develop its own leadership, standards, norms, and methods of interaction over time. Groups can be used over an entire semester or they can meet for 10-20 minutes during a single class session, depending on the course design.

Groups are often used in the behavioral and social sciences, including business. They can be used with advantage in the humanities and the sciences if the small group session is well planned and the purpose for forming the group is clear to the members.

How

Divide a large class into the required number of five- to seven-member groups. This can be done by pointing to specific students, by grouping surnames from the attendance sheet, or by sounding off. As an example of sounding off, if the class is to be divided into eight groups of five students each, have the students, in sequence, number themselves from one to five, repeating this sequence eight times. Then those eight students who have number one gather in one spot, while the eight students who have number two gather in a different spot, etc.

In some cases, having students self select their own groups, which may then vary in size, is a useful and efficient method of group formation. This method eliminates complaints to the professor about non-contributing students and usually results in closer cooperation among group members and more self policing of individual efforts.

Locate each group so that the groups are reasonably separate, but minimize the class time spent in dividing and locating.

Specify the topic each group is to discuss or to research, the length of time available for work in class, and the product the group is to develop as a result of its efforts. Groups may all work on the same problem (competition is occasionally useful), on different problems, or on different aspects of a larger problem.

For in-class discussion groups, float from group to group, observing and listening. Be certain that the class has the informational basis for the group task. Be prepared to intervene to keep the group on track, to clarify points, and to answer questions. The professor may wish to use a point raised by a specific group for clarification to the entire class.

For groups working together on a research project, have the group leader or each individual write periodic progress reports. Individual progress reports can check the contributions that each member is making to the project.

At some point, depending on whether the small group has been formed for an in-class discussion or for a longer-term research project, the class will benefit from hearing a report about the results of other discussions and projects. Each group should choose a spokesperson to summarize its results to the class and to answer questions from other class members about its efforts. A reasonable time limit should be set and adhered to for these summaries. Students who exceed the time limits for the summaries should expect to be cut off. However, the time allowed for questions may be flexible, depending on the interest of the class and the time available.

Advantages

- Provides an opportunity for each student to participate.
- Increases probability of involvement and contribution by reticent class members.
- Reduces the impact of class "stars."
- Enables a wider subject range to be covered more intensively than in general discussion or question-and-answer.
- Enables individual opinions to be shared in a less threatening environment.
- Helps to clarify points not readily understood.
- Enables students to apply concepts presented in class.
- Encourages problem solving.
- Facilitates review sessions.

Disadvantages

- Time used to form groups may be wasteful.
- Method requires experience for use in large (>100) classes.
- Method is not suitable for classes with fixed seats (i.e., amphitheaters, etc.).
- Classroom may not have enough space for sufficient separation between discussion groups.
- Information shared may not be accurate.
- Some students may not "pull their own weight" in the group and cause dissatisfaction and morale problems.
- Groups may progress unevenly both in time required to complete the assignment and in the quality of the content.

Recommendations

Small groups may be used to encourage participation by all students in a well-focused discussion or in a well-structured research project. They are particularly useful for applying learning, for problem solving, and for review sessions.

5. OTHER GROUP TECHNIQUES

☐ **CIRCLE:** A circle can be used in small classes and in seminars where the chairs can be arranged easily.

How

Arrange chairs in a circle, being careful that this is easy to do and does not take much time. Be certain that the class is small and that conversational, face-to-face discussion will achieve the goals and objectives for the class.

Advantages

- Encourages face-to-face communication among students.
- Tends to make the professor more a member of the group.
- Is more conversational, yet otherwise the same as a small group (see 4. Small Groups).
- Benefits discussion-oriented classes.

Disadvantages

- Note taking is difficult.
- Some time may be wasted in arranging the circle.
- Small group disadvantages also apply.

Recommendations

Use circles to encourage maximum student participation in small classes when participation is part of the learning. Circles are particularly appropriate for foreign-language classes. Check the disadvantages of the small group method so you do not use the method inappropriately.

☐ **FISHBOWL:** In the fishbowl a small group forms a circle and discusses a topic while the rest of the class forms an audience in secondary rows around the circle and observes.

How

Decide how many class members to include in the small group. Be certain that the chairs in the classroom are not fixed in position and that sufficient space is available for the fishbowl arrangement of a circle and secondary rows for the rest of the class. You can vary the arrangement by designating one chair in the fishbowl circle as a temporary one to be used by various "observers" from the secondary rows who will take turns in joining the fishbowl group.

Advantages

- Optimizes learning when the act of observing is a behavioral objective.
- Enables entire class to be part of the same discussion.
- Provides variety to stimulate learning in larger classes.

Disadvantages

- Participants usually learn more than the observers.

- Class time may be wasted in setting up the fishbowl.

Recommendations

Use when the act of observing is a behavioral objective. Also use when the class is too large for a circle but when the course objectives require one.

☐ **INSTRUMENTED SMALL GROUPS:** This method serves to focus and to lead discussions. The instrument may be a written problem, a puzzle, an artifact, etc. This method is only as effective as the instrument is relevant to the objective to be achieved.

How

Choose an instrument relevant to the problem. For instance, a geology class may be asked to identify a particular rock sample, a computer science class may be asked to decode a program, etc.

Advantages

- Applies conceptual learning to practical situations.
- Brings the real world into the classroom.
- Enhances student interest in a conceptual subject.

Disadvantages

- Student solutions may be more "creative" than practical.
- Students may not have learned enough to discuss or to solve the problem.
- Relevant instruments are often difficult to obtain.
- Students from a prior term may communicate solutions to students in the current class.

Recommendations

This can be a valuable method if the students have sufficient knowledge and background. The method is often used in high schools. It should not be repeated using the same instrument in consecutive academic terms.

☐ **BRAINSTORMING:** Brainstorming is a method developed by industry to generate new ideas. The method tends to be both misused and overused. Brainstorming is an initial step in problem solving by uncritically generating as many ideas as possible. Each person's ideas may suggest ideas to other members of the brainstorming group. After brainstorming, the ideas generated are grouped, which may lead to even more ideas. Only then are the ideas ranked and criticized. Usually most ideas are immediately discarded; however, a few may be original and interesting to pursue. The goal is to generate as many ideas as possible in the shortest period of time by having group members build on each other's suggestions. The group must remain loose and uncritical of the ideas generated during the actual brainstorming period, saving criticism for later review and evaluation of the ideas.

How

Give the group clear instructions on the brainstorming process, emphasizing that the ideas are not to be criticized or developed during the brainstorming period. Specify a 10-20 minute time period and immediately cut off the brainstorming when the specified time is reached. Review and evaluate the ideas by first grouping them in general topic areas, if necessary, then ranking each idea within a topic area according to its value for further discussion. Develop ideas that seem useful, analyzing and criticizing these ideas in relation to the goals or the purpose of the brainstorming session.

Other ways of handling ideas generated by brainstorming may be considered. The process described above is the most common way.

Advantages

- Generates many ideas very quickly.
- Provides input to further discussion and problem solving.
- Involves everyone in the group.
- Can be fun.
- Encourages creativity.
- May be used to generate a research problem in a research-oriented class.

Disadvantages

- Students must know enough about the subject to generate relevant ideas.
- The method has limited use in a classroom situation.

Recommendations

This method is an excellent stimulus to creativity where many heads are better than one, provided that the students know enough about the subject to generate ideas relevant to the topic being brainstormed.

6. QUESTION-AND-ANSWER

Question-and-answer in this book refers to questions by students or to questions by the professor. Questions by students may range from asking for a brief clarification of a point made in class to a whole class session devoted to student questions. Questions by the professor may have a similar range.

Questions help students to think during the class session and force them to organize and state a response. A student can be led, with questions, to develop a point. Questions can help the student to focus on important points.

In preparing for question-and-answer sessions in which the professor is to formulate the questions, review the comments above regarding planning for discussion sessions. Question-and-answer sessions may be used to determine the students' level of understanding of various points, to determine knowledge based on outside reading, and to elucidate connections between various ideas. They are especially useful at the stage in the semester when it is appropriate to pause, review, and synthesize material covered in class, assignments, and laboratory. They are also useful in courses where students have been working independently on different problems or readings to show the connections among them.

Sessions devoted to questions by students are appropriate for clarifying student understanding of various points. If one student asks a question about an unclear point, other students are probably unclear about that point too. While answering a lot of questions during presentation of subject material interrupts the flow (especially if the question is tangential to the subject), questions are an indicator of student involvement in the subject and also of their comfort level in interacting with the professor. Setting aside a part or parts of a class session for question answering can reassure students of the professor's interest in reducing any discomfort they may have about a point or an assignment. Frequently, question-and-answer sessions occur at the beginning of a class to clear up any questions from the last class or from assignments. Question-and-answer sessions may also occur at the end of the class to clear up points raised during the class and about any forthcoming assignments.

It is important to have in mind how much time to devote solely to questions and answers because they can be time consuming. Occasionally, students will use them as a stalling procedure. In a 50-minute class, 5 minutes at the beginning and 10 minutes at the end might be appropriate. Longer question-and-answer sessions are appropriate for review classes before a major test or exam.

The professor should realize that question-and-answer is seductive as well as comfortable because it becomes a conversational method of presentation. Although answers to student questions can be kept relevant to the subject, they can often become more advanced or more detailed than necessary for the goals and objectives of the course. The professor must keep these goals and objectives in mind. On the other hand, the professor should not be so rigid that student questions that raise interesting asides go unanswered.

Questions from the professor keep students alert and on their toes. However, the professor should refrain from embarrassing the anxious, shy, or ill-prepared student.

How

Try to rotate questions among students and to give priority to the student who asks questions least frequently. Time spent on questions may be limited to the beginning and the end of class. Focus answers to questions on subject matter, especially as the questions relate to the goals and objectives of the course.

One effective way to use questions and answers involves having the students write several questions which they think would be appropriate to be asked on a forthcoming test or examination. This provides feedback for the teacher about what has been learned and what the students feel has been emphasized or is important. It also facilitates test construction and provides a basis for reviewing the subject. In general, students come up with more difficult and more specific questions than the teacher would!

When the professor asks the questions, she should try to make the questions provocative and worth class time. Focus the questions on the material the students are supposed to have learned or to be in the process of learning.

Advantages
- Facilitates interaction between students and professor.
- Can be lively when well paced.
- Clarifies and reviews subject material.
- Checks on assignments.
- Provides student feedback on unclear points.
- Emphasizes professor's important points.
- Assists in constructing reviews and exams.

Disadvantages
- Student questions often have no focus or organization.

- Prepared and/or verbal students have an advantage.
- Time may be wasted with irrelevant questions.
- Less material can be covered than with other methods.

Recommendations

Question-and-answer is and should be part of any course, if not every session. It provides valuable student feedback and an effective way to check on student progress, although it favors the well-prepared and/or verbal student.

7. DEBATE

Debate may be used to present issues which have no specific answer. These issues include the areas of public policy, cultural mores, and ethics. *Note*: Debate is widely used in speech and communication studies, but this use is not addressed here. Students should feel strongly about the topic selected for debate. At the same time, they should not feel so strongly that they cannot accept information about an opinion with which they differ.

How

Select a topic which has no specific correct or feasible answer, but which can be debated both positively and negatively. Sometimes an appropriate topic will arise in group discussion. The professor or the students then select teams to prepare informational material about the topic. One team will prepare information to support a favorable position about the topic. Another team will prepare information to support a position opposing the topic. A representative from each team must be selected to lead the debate. The class time allotted for the debate must be specified. It may be followed by formal questions and answers addressed to the debators. The class then votes on the debate topic. For a 50-minute class, limit the debate to 30 minutes, leaving 10-15 minutes for questions and 5 minutes for the vote.

Advantages
- Provokes lively arguments.
- Serves to illuminate two sides of an issue.
- Summarizes two sides of an issue.
- Adds variety and student involvement to the subject.

Disadvantages
- Students may emphasize style over substance.
- Debators usually learn more than their listeners.

- The debate topic may be seen as more important than it is in relation to other topics in the course.
- Opinions are often polarized.
- A topic with a range of possible responses is discussed in terms of only two opposing responses.
- Emotions often overwhelm the ability to accept information.
- Applicability is limited.

Recommendations

Debates are useful for polarized or polarizing issues. The debate will highlight these issues, but ignore a range of other possible responses to the issue. The debate may also, in the minds of students, overemphasize one course topic to the detriment of others.

8. CASE METHOD

The Harvard Business School popularized the case method, which is now widely used in law and business schools. The method deserves wider application. There are many kinds of cases. Westmeyer lists six: incident, issue, description, individual, historical, and research (p 70). Learning goals for using cases differ. Westmeyer differentiates between cases:

1) To teach content
2) To teach principles
3) To discover precedents
4) To teach techniques
5) To teach decision making
6) To make decisions on current problems
7) To teach attitudes (Westmeyer, p 71).

How

An example or case from actual practice is introduced for in-depth student analysis. The students have an opportunity to apply the concepts and methods they have learned, as well as the jargon, to solving the problems that the case presents. At the same time, the professor acts as the devil's advocate by pointing out difficulties and inconsistencies in the student approach to solving the problem the case presents. At times, this role of the devil's advocate can also be used to examine student learning.

The case method can also be used in classes involving management or administration as a way of enabling students to set work priorities. The student is given an "in-basket" with a set of documents that must be acted upon in a specified time period. The student's problem is to prioritize the action-requiring documents and to explain why each was assigned a particular priority level.

Advantages

- Provides an opportunity to apply conceptual learning to a practical situation.
- Demonstrates real-life situations.
- Involves students in decision making.
- Evaluates specific abilities.

Disadvantages

- Students need a base of knowledge to apply to the case at hand.
- Cases must be carefully selected to illustrate important situations and points.
- Student network may provide "best answers" when cases are frequently repeated from term to term.

Recommendations

For students who already have a knowledge base in a subject area, the case method provides a reality-based opportunity to analyze, synthesize, and apply their learning. The method is especially useful in applied or technical fields of study and for mature students with job experience.

9. WORDS-METHODS-THEORIES

Words-Methods-Theories is a unique approach to presenting introductory material. It is based on the idea that a subject is really interesting only when a student knows enough to work with it. With introductory material—the first encounter with subject matter—the student may not be able to read or understand, much less to comprehend more detailed articles on the subject. The student does not yet possess the jargon of the field, does not know the methods used, or the pertinent models and theories that define a particular area of knowledge. The subject expert or scholar, on the other hand, is immured to jargon and may not even recognize that he or she is using language unfamiliar to students and making assumptions about approaches to knowledge that the student has not yet acquired. Each subject area has its own language or way of using terminology. Students are easily and understandably confused when ordinary English language words take on completely different meanings and connotations within a specific subject area. Professors are so familiar with the specialized usages in their subject areas that they may not be aware how confusing the language is for the uninitiated. Learning the language of a subject area becomes part of the acculturation process for the student.

How

In presenting introductory material about a new subject, use the Berlitz method of talking in the language while, at the same time, telling stories about uses and applications of the subject, with interesting asides. Attempt a lot of description while presenting the same topic from different points of view, always in the language of the subject area. You can joke about the terminology, but always use the new terms repeatedly. The goal is to enable the students to feel comfortable enough with the new language to speak it too. Only then will the students feel comfortable reading texts and articles by practitioners in the subject area.

Names of models, methods, and theories employed by the particular subject area should be included on the course outline for reinforcement and emphasis. Glossaries may be included but only for reference, not for memorization as if they were grade school spelling lists. An early quiz about the words, methods, and theories after six weeks may be a minor percentage of the term grade and provide feedback about student learning. Such a quiz should be composed of the following kinds of questions:

- Describe a certain method or theory
- Define a particular term
- Fill-in-the-blank with an appropriate word
- Match related items.

The student who can pass this kind of test can understand the basic concepts and language in a new subject area. Students whose dominant language is not English often have an advantage with introductory material in a new subject area. They expect that the language is going to be difficult and focus on vocabulary. Students whose dominant language is English are often frustrated and initially turned off by material written in unfamiliar terminology, which makes assumptions about key ideas to which the student has not yet been exposed.

The key ideas, methods, and theories in a subject area serve to unite a large body of facts into a meaningful whole. As the facts fall into place they become logical and obvious examples that are easy to remember. The Words-Method-Theories method to introduce a new subject area quickly makes a subject meaningful and enables new facts to be placed in a logical structure where they are easy to remember.

Advantages
- Makes a new subject area quickly meaningful.
- Responds to student needs for background information prior to in-depth study.
- Gives professor a structured method to introduce a new subject area.

Disadvantages
- Students may be bored.
- Students may be trapped into rote learning.

Recommendations
Focusing on the words, methods, and theories in a new subject area serves to emphasize their importance as an integral part of the field. Although the method is useful for introducing a subject, students may require a whole program of study to work with the words, methods, and theories introduced.

10. LECTURE-DISCUSSION

There are many ways to conduct a lecture-discussion class. Most are combinations of the other methods suggested here. The following is but one way of doing it.

How
Lecture for not more than 20 minutes of the class hour, then shift to discussion (small group or total group). Pose a problem or issue. Students use the information (data, model, theory, method of analysis) to solve one or more relevant examples. The professor critiques the process as it goes along. At the end, the professor summarizes the important points.

Advantages
- Discussion is based on information presented in the lecture.
- Discussion is specific and directed.
- Opportunity to immediately determine if students understand points made and can apply them.
- Students actively participate.

• Good introduction to an assignment that requires an essay response.

Disadvantages

• May tend to fragment learning.
• Discussion may be too short to solve problem.

An alternative is for students to respond individually in writing for about 10 minutes and then get together to discuss their initial responses. This variation may involve each student and reduce the tendency to depend on the stronger (or more awake) students for responses.

Recommendations

Lecture-discussion provides an opportunity for professors to immediately probe the students' level of understanding and elucidate the topic. It also focuses students on the lecture topic, its importance, and use.

11. SIMULATIONS AND GAMES

Simulations and games have long been used primarily in the social sciences. Role play is a common example. Simulations and games are being used with increasing frequency for computer-assisted learning in the natural and mathematical sciences. Simulations and games both involve a complex set of interacting variables to be abstracted from a real situation or from a type of activity. These variables are represented symbolically. They can also be represented mathematically to facilitate computer manipulation.

Simulations and games are available in a number of subject areas. They vary in quality and in applicability to a given class situation. However, they are a very effective method of "learning by doing," which actively involves the student. Simulations and games, better than most methods, show how the manipulation of certain variables can affect a whole system. The time spent in designing a game or simulation is worthwhile.

How

Vendor catalogs and evaluative literature are a source of many games and simulations proven effective for various subject areas. The professor can also design her own. The simulation or game should show how a system is affected by manipulating specified variables in certain ways. It should also allow trial and error manipulation to demonstrate the effects of improper actions.

Advantages

- Presents most effectively a large number of complex variables interacting within a system.
- Involves students in "learning by doing."
- Demonstrates the results of incorrect as well as correct actions.
- Uses student and professorial time efficiently.

Disadvantages

- Time for completion frequently exceeds the class period.
- Often more appropriate for individualized instruction than for a classroom situation.
- Often requires special equipment or computers with adequate memory.
- Requirements of special equipment may limit number of students who can use the simulation or game.

Recommendations

The use of simulations and games should be encouraged where appropriate to the course objectives and where time and technology allow.

12. PANELS

A panel of experts can introduce students to people who represent several points of view in discussing the same subject. Panels can be used with students as an alternative to the debate method.

How

Invite three to five outside speakers to serve on a panel or assign a panel of three to five students to investigate a topic from different points of view. Define the topic carefully, especially for student panels. Students will need guidance to prepare a well-defined point of view. Outside speakers serving on a panel will require less topic definition. However, they should know the level and sophistication of the class, and the professor should tell them what has already been covered in the course.

All panelists should know the length of time allotted for their presentation and be aware that they will be cut off should they run overtime. The professor should moderate the panel or appoint a moderator from among the panel members. The moderator's first job is to introduce each panel member, giving a brief background for an outside speaker and a brief title for each presentation. Following the presentations, the moderator conducts a question-and-answer period during which students forming the audience can direct specific questions to one panelist or to the panel as a whole. The moderator should not allow one panelist to dominate the discussion. At the end of the class period, the moderator (especially one who is also the professor) may wish to summarize the session. Alternatively, the moderator may wish to summarize the session before taking questions from students in the audience.

In the class session following the panel, the professor may wish to summarize, once again, the panel discussion and the question-and-answer period, emphasizing points covered and relating these points to the subject matter of the course.

Advantages
- Engages student interest.
- Provides a range of views and opinions.
- Presents authoritative and data-driven opinions.

Disadvantages
- Coordinating panelists' time schedules is difficult.
- Preparation and presentation are time consuming.

Recommendations
The panel takes a lot of planning and coordination in order to present a diverse range of opinions. If the panel succeeds, much learning can occur. If panelists do not show up or are ill prepared, the time invested in preparation may be wasted in terms of learning achieved.

13. TEAM TEACHING

Team teaching can be stimulating for teachers and students alike. The team consists of teachers representing various viewpoints, if not disciplines, working as a synergistic group. Team teaching is an especially good learning-management method for interdisciplinary areas such as cognitive science. Professors in this area might be drawn from psychology, philosophy, linguistics, neurology, neurochemistry, computer science, etc.

Team teaching presents similar difficulties to those inherent in coordinating and scheduling outside speakers for a panel discussion. Adding to these difficulties, professors from different fields will have their own jargons, methodologies, and theories that are unfamiliar to professors in other fields and which are clearly unfamiliar to students. Building a teaching team is indeed difficult for the faculty involved; it is equally difficult for the students who are supposed to benefit from the team-teaching approach.

Building a teaching team is time consuming. It requires a group of interacting faculty who are committed to giving and receiving information, building on each other's ideas, and clearing up any communications difficulties on an ongoing basis. Team teaching involves sublimating individual egos and goals to those of the group. A two- or three-person team usually works together more easily than a six- or eight-person team. Ideally, the team should have lots of opportunity for daily informal communication and idea sharing. The availability of a team of teachers makes possible a variety of teaching styles and presentation methods.

How

The faculty team must agree on course goals and objectives, course design, presentation, and evaluation methods. The team must select a coordinator responsible for administrative details such as calling team meetings, arranging for support materials, keeping track of student assignments, faculty assignments for evaluation of student work, and grading. Individual team members must be scheduled to present each segment of the course. Ideally, each team member attends all classes as both a primary presentor and as a secondary resource. This makes it easier to integrate segments, to provide continuity, and to discuss the same topic from several points of view. Designing a team-taught course involves considerable time commitment. Once the course begins, the team should meet frequently to review class sessions, to give feedback to individual team members who have conducted particular class sessions, to monitor the progress of both the course and individual students, and to fine tune the course.

Note: Guest lectures in a course by faculty members not responsible for the course content do not constitute team teaching as described above. The guest lecturer presents material from his or her own field without detailed knowledge of the class and, generally, on a one-class or part-of-a-class basis.

Advantages

• Helps students to see the relationships between diverse disciplines.

• Provides a role model for cooperative efforts.

• Stimulates thought among team members as each builds on another's ideas.

• Develops collegiality when working well.

Disadvantages

• Students can be confused when inadequate planning results in a variety of jargons and references to seemingly unrelated methods and theories.

• Teaching often deteriorates after the course has been given a few times because professors lose initial enthusiasm and are unwilling to devote the time required.

• Time consuming for team members, often without adequate remuneration for additional effort involved.

• Because team members rarely receive full course load credit, administration becomes a difficult problem.

Recommendations

Team teaching is especially valuable for interdisciplinary subjects but can be used to present any subject. The school must be ready to commit the resources (faculty time) required, and the faculty must be ready to commit a major effort to course planning and evaluation.

14. DEMONSTRATIONS

Demonstrations are familiar in the sciences and should, perhaps, be more widely employed in the social sciences and the humanities. They are used to show processes—how things happen. They are also used to show techniques and instrumentation. They make abstractions concrete. They complement lectures and discussion as important and widely used methods of classroom presentation. They can hone observational skills. They can provide raw data for analysis and synthesis. Devising new, appropriate, and directed demonstrations in a subject area is one of the many creative activities open to the professor.

How

In devising the demonstration, be clear about its purpose, e.g., to sharpen observational skills, to illustrate, to show technique. Practice the demonstration to make sure that it works. Visualize the class observing the demonstration—even though you've done it over and over, you will do it differently in front of the class. Once the demonstration has been devised, its presentation in front of a class becomes a process in itself with the following sequence of steps:

• Arrive early for class with all the necessary equipment and with backups. Murphy's Law (anything that can go wrong will go wrong and at the worst possible time) is infallible when demonstrating before a group;

• Recheck all the materials and equipment to be sure they are in working order and ready to be used in the required order;

• Describe to the class what and how you are going to demonstrate;

• Proceed with the demonstration, explaining the process as you are demonstrating it;

• Explain what the demonstration accomplished and what was required for it to succeed;

• Place the demonstration in the context of the course objectives.

Demonstrations need to receive the same care in preparation as lectures. They are essential for clear presentation of certain kinds of information and to enhance comprehension and understanding of other kinds of information.

For large classes, TV monitors, if available, may be useful. Although they take away from the immediacy of first-hand observation, they enable students far from the demonstration to grasp details they would be otherwise unable to see. Closed-circuit TV is available on some campuses to assist demonstrations to large classes. The audio-visual or media department can assist with its implementation.

Any time technology such as closed-circuit TV is considered, the possibility of pre-taping the demonstration should be considered. Pre-taping has the advantage of ensuring a flawless demonstration. The taping can be repeated as often as necessary to achieve the quality level desired for the demonstration. The tape can then be saved and used over again as required. Pre-taping is time consuming (the first-time professor will probably not have time to invest in this activity), but worth the investment in the long run. When using TV technology, be mindful that students are accustomed to the quality of commercial broadcasting. In addition, they have also learned to tune out or ignore the television set. Copies of taped demonstrations available for general use may often be found in the library. The media department is well worth investigating for this type of material.

One-Way Vision Rooms

One-way vision rooms are often available for demonstrations, especially in psychology. Requirements for scheduling a class into a one-way vision room should be determined.

Advantages

• Makes the abstract concrete.

- Shows instrumentation in action.
- Shows phenomena in action.
- Trains observational skills.
- Provides data for analysis.
- Illustrates sequential processes.
- Illustrates examples that led to theories and models.

Disadvantages

- Lengthy demonstrations or dramatic demonstrations may unbalance the course design and interrupt the flow.
- May require more preparation than action.

Recommendations

Integrate demonstrations creatively into the course design to show process or technique and to teach observational skills. Be careful that highly successful or dramatic demonstration does not unbalance the course content in student minds.

15. SEMINARS

A seminar is referred to here as an in-depth study with a small group of students (e.g., 8-10). Seminars present an opportunity for extensive literature or research study; they are widely used for upper-level undergraduates, masters, and doctoral students.

There are many ways of conducting such study. One is detailed study of research, in which selected studies are analyzed in depth. Another is along the lines of "Current Readings in......" A third might be advanced analysis of a particular author's work, a particular style, or theory. Two of the many methods are discussed below.

☐ **LITERATURE SEMINARS:** In one type of literature seminar each student selects aspects of a subject and presents seminar papers in the class session. These are then discussed. Ordinarily each student presents three or four seminar papers, although this varies depending on the level of the student and the subject area.

How

The first seminar session comprises a review of assumed background, presentation of the topic areas to be covered, selection and scheduling of student presentations, specification of expected academic standards, and presentation format. Begin the first seminar session by reviewing base information, i.e., any information that is assumed as a basis for the course. Seminars are usually designed for third-level students who have had at least first- and second-level courses in the subject area. The review may be conducted by the professor, by question-and-answer, discussion, or by having several students assigned to provide state-of-the-art reviews for the second and third seminar sessions.

Delineate broad topic areas to be covered in the course. Have students select specific aspects to study and present to the seminar group. The professor may provide a suggested list, the students may generate the list, or each student may select, with the professor's approval, aspects of particular interest.

Assign the session at which each presentation is to be made, having the presentations form a logical order. Do not permit late presentations; lateness is no more permissible at this level of study than in the work environment or at professional meetings. Indicate minimal acceptable standards for specificity of study and the professor's expectation level. Time limits for oral presentations vary with the subject and with the seminar period; however, equal time should be given to the presentation and to the discussion period following the presentation. Make clear whether or not a formal, written seminar paper is required for each presentation. Custom varies from requiring a written paper for each presentation to requiring only the presentation itself. The professor may assume that third-level students in a seminar oriented to research literature should know how to avail themselves of the reference and computerized searching services of a college or university library. However, the student may not be aware of some of the sources most relevant to the seminar topic. The professor may wish to have a list of these sources, including abstracting and indexing sources, to hand out to seminar participants.

A useful format requires students to make copies of seminar papers available before their presentation to other members of the class, including the professor. Having the papers to read before the presentation enables more informed discussion. The presentation then becomes a short summary with elucidation and discussion of interesting points raised by the material.

After the first session, subsequent ones follow the format of presentation, discussion, and professorial critique. The professor adds other interesting research and points out areas that need further research and investigation. This information is particularly valuable for students looking forward to theses and dissertations. The professor should also guide the seminar participants to see how the various topics presented relate to and are integrated into the overall subject matter of the course.

Advantages

- Provides students with an in-depth knowledge of a subject area.
- Provides practical experience in synthesizing scattered information on a topic of interest.
- Enables the student to experience state-of-the-art reviewing.
- Establishes professional performance standards.
- Provides experience giving oral presentations.

Disadvantages

- Presentations may be uneven in quality of content.
- Early presentations may not be as thoroughly prepared as later ones, causing difficulties in evaluation.
- Oral presentations may be difficult for some students.

Recommendations

Seminars are a valuable way for students to gain in-depth knowledge of a subject and to communicate and discuss this knowledge with other seminar participants. The students learn from each other while the professor guides and adds to the information presented. Seminars are less valuable for weak students than for strong ones looking forward to graduate school or involved in a graduate program.

☐ **RESEARCH METHODS SEMINARS:** Research seminars are designed to discuss research in a small group with feedback from an experienced research-oriented professor. The purpose of a research seminar may range from learning how to do research in a specific subject area to reviewing the research literature of a specific field to reviewing and discussing research in progress. Seminars designed to review the research literature have been described in the previous section.

Research methods seminars to develop an acceptable research proposal may follow a research methodology course. In general, students need help in refining a problem area into a manageable research project. This help includes guidance in defining the problem and developing working hypotheses, insuring a complete literature search, devising a relevant and valid methodology using appropriate statistics, and writing the research proposal.

How

The student's work, depending on the type of problem, should be scheduled to present a preliminary proposal approximately two weeks before the end of the term. The student then has time to revise the proposal before submitting it in final form at the last seminar session. The major areas of difficulty often arise in defining a manageable problem and in devising relevant methodology and measures to investigate it. Discussing and refining student ideas as the students investigate relevant and related research reports should be balanced with instruction in proposal writing. In general, if few students have had experience with proposal writing, the professor might provide some acceptable models for students to examine.

Advantages

- Guides the student in initial major research efforts.
- Provides a structure for developing an acceptable research proposal.
- Insures that institutional research standards are upheld.

Disadvantages

- The time-frame of the course may prove counter productive to developing a well-developed research proposal.
- The professor may not be able to devote sufficient time within the time-frame of the course to effectively assist each student.

Recommendations

While some colleges and universities schedule research methods seminars to assist in proposal development, the time-frame of the course may not match the pace required for all proposals. Some excellent potential researchers may drop out, and some weaker ones may propose an easy-to-solve problem to successfully complete the course.

16. ON-SITE CLASSES

Sometimes it is appropriate for one or more sessions of a class to meet at some place other than the usual classroom. The class might meet at a museum, computer center, or library. Certain classes might meet at places appropriate to the subject, such as an astronomy class at the observatory, a psychology class at the child study center, a botany class at an arboretum and so on.

On campus on-site meetings are often appropriate. Off campus meetings require that time to travel to and from the site not interfere with other classes or activities.

This section refers to presentation of material to a group rather than to individual students. Laboratory study is discussed in the Laboratory chapter. Use on-site classes when a demonstration is not adequate to the purpose. Do not use for on-site guest lectures; arrange for guest lecturers to come to the regular classroom.

How

• Schedule the class session, preferably giving the date and the site on the syllabus.

• Confirm the visit with personnel at the site.

• Remind the class during the session immediately before the visit.

• Introduce what is to be seen or done; put in context with other class work; raise questions the students should be asking themselves during the visit to focus the learning.

• Make an advance visit to the site before scheduling it. Discuss quite specifically the purposes-objectives to be met etc., with person who will conduct the session. In other words, the on-site class is more than an unfocused field trip or a way of getting someone else to do your (the professor's) work.

• Summarize at the end.

• In the next class, relate the visit to the context of the course. Solicit reactions by class discussion or by assignment.

Advantages

• Can be used for demonstrations that cannot be brought into class.

• May be used for material that needs to be discussed, questioned, and clarified during observation.

• Provides a real situation.

• May be used to introduce an assignment.

• Enables a change of pace.

Disadvantages

• Time required may be disproportionate to the learning.

• Difficult to evaluate the actual learning that takes place.

• May cause loss of course momentum.

Recommendations

Use on-site study when important and necessary to course design.

17. MINI-LABS AND WORKSHOPS

There are a number of situations that justify students spending class time individually or in small groups examining or manipulating the material of the field that do not justify having on-going laboratory sessions. There are also cases where activities ordinarily done as outside assignments can be done (or started) in class. In the case of mini-labs the goal is to show the students how to perform or how to study the material on their own. In workshops the goal is how to perform or accomplish, e.g., a writing exercise or problem-solving. The students may work individually, in pairs, or in small groups. These situations require instructor elucidation, comment, guidance, and immediate feedback. Some examples are: (1) examination and manipulation of a concordance database by mini-computer for an English class; (2) writing kanji for a Japanese language class; (3) examination of cultural artifacts for a history or anthropology course.

How

• Prepare instructions for what to do and questions to be answered.

• Obtain material or data.

• In class, give oral instructions for the task. Help students individually or have students trade data and responses and critique each other.

18. COMMITTEE OR PROJECT CLASS

Another increasingly popular method is to devote time to solving real-life problems. For example, a social science class might work on a community issue, an engineering class might have teams develop workable products, a management class might help a small company, an architecture class might design a building for community use—such as a geriatric facility, and so forth. Such emphases have the potential of putting the learning in context, making it meaningful, and generating motivation and enthusiasm.

This technique differs from using design or application as a term project in that the professor's organization and presentation of material is structured around problem solution. The presentation focus is on what information is required, how to find the information, how to evaluate the information, considerations in design, decision-making among alternatives, evaluating potential solutions, interacting with community groups or purchasers, etc. Students take responsibility for learning about the subject outside of class and reporting on content in class.

Such classes might take the form of committee meetings with the professor taking the role of expert consultant.

19. PEER TEACHING

Peer teaching has been receiving increasing emphasis. The idea is to personalize and individualize instruction, particularly in large classes. There are three main types of peer teaching: (1) discussion groups, seminars, or tutorials conducted by student assistants, (2) the proctor model used in Personalized Systems of Instruction (see Laboratory chapter) by senior students, and (3) student learning groups. Dunkin and Barnes review peer teaching and conclude that at its best it encourages students to take responsibility for their own learning and that it should not be used alone (Dunkin and Barnes).

20. OPTIONS FOR VERY LARGE CLASSES

The professor may be faced with the problem of how to individualize and personalize very large classes as well as provide opportunities for the advantages of discussion methods. The following have been used:

- Traditional lectures
- Lecture with discussion sections
- Lecture with individual study groups
- TV, cable, or videotape lectures with discussion sections
- Individual learning methods with discussion sections
- Computer-assisted learning.

21. OPTIONS FOR VERY SMALL CLASSES

Very small classes provide options for individualizing and personalizing instruction. The following may be used to supplement or replace some class sessions:

- Tutorials
- Individual learning methods
- Conference
- Meeting in different sites
- Field trips
- Computer methods including conferencing and electronic mail.

22. SHORT COURSES

Short courses provide an opportunity for intensive study of a subject. Often the short course is the only course the student is taking at the time. Short courses are commonly offered in the summer, in inter-session or in a special winter term. A short course with full credit should have the same number of contact hours and the same amount of assignment and laboratory as regular courses. This is the assumption under which such courses are accredited.

Intensive study may be an advantage in certain subjects such as languages. Students like the opportunity to devote total time to a single subject. Other courses that require extended thinking about the subject over time may result in intellectual indigestion if offered as a short course. These are best offered in regular term.

USING MEDIA

The use of photographic and electronic media has enhanced classroom presentation. Using the newer media, evaluated and selected by the professor to achieve specific course objectives, the student can have a variety of learning experiences not otherwise possible. The development of courseware for use with a computer is currently revolutionizing teaching in many areas. In years to come, well-developed courseware will be as common a teaching tool as the overhead projector, slides, and film are today.

The simplest aids are the chalkboard and handouts. The chalkboard is used frequently to emphasize a point, spell an unfamiliar term or name, develop arguments, and derive equations. However, when there is a great deal of material, a handout may be preferable. The experienced professor has learned to carry chalk (especially at the end of the semester).

When the equipment is unfamiliar, get a lesson in operation from the media department. Order any necessary equipment in advance, including such things as a screen and extension cord, for a specific classroom. Check 10 minutes before class to see that the equipment is ready. When an equipment failure occurs during class, call on skills within the classroom; often there are students familiar with the equipment. Continue with the class or use an alternative presentation when necessary. An A/V aide who can attend to the equipment while the professor is conducting the class is often helpful.

Use the proper medium for the purpose. Do not expect students to take accurate notes from crowded material on a slide or the chalkboard. Use a handout instead. Avoid a long audio recording or a poor video such as "talking heads."

Using more than one medium in a single class period requires smooth transitions. Learning media should be an aid and auxiliary to effective presentation rather than an interruption to a class.

1. OVERHEAD PROJECTOR: TRANSPARENCIES

An overhead projector is used for 8 1/2" x 11" transparencies, sometimes called slides. The transparencies may be produced by the professor, written or drawn during a classroom session, or purchased. Transparencies can also be produced from computer graphics. They may be made in different colors and overlaid on one another. Ideally, as an argument is developed, strikingly effective uses can be made of overlaid transparencies. Transparencies are effective for line drawing, schematics, and for a limited quantity of text no smaller than the capitals on a primary typewriter.

How

If the classroom is not provided with an overhead projector, with prior planning one can generally be obtained from the media department. The classroom should also have a screen, although a blank, smooth white wall can be utilized effectively. Transparencies on various subjects may be part of the media center collection. However, transparencies can easily be made on many photocopy machines. For details on this process, consult the media center or the secretarial support staff for the program. Purchased transparencies are often in color. Special pens are available in basic colors for self-produced transparencies. (In a pinch, these pens used on a transparent plastic bag make a satisfactory substitute for a more professional product.) Transparencies stored in a file or folder should each be separated by a piece of white paper. This facilitates review and avoids smearing. Unmounted transparencies (those not surrounded by a piece of poster board) can be easily placed in a folder. Replace each transparency after use for ease in retrieval for further use or review.

When showing a transparency to a class, stand to the side of the projector. A sharpened pencil or a pen pointed to the particular aspect of the transparency the professor wishes to emphasize makes a useful and unobtrusive pointer. Remember to talk to the class, not to the transparency.

Advantages

Transparencies are inexpensive, easy to make, and can be reused. Overhead projectors are readily available. Transparencies can be used as a guide for major points to be made during a lecture. Transparencies can also be used for graphics and for writing mathematical formulae, saving much chalkboard writing time and making a more effective, professional presentation of course material. Transparencies can also be used to supplement and to complement material on the chalkboard.

Transparencies can be carried in the ordinary brief case, stored in file drawers, reviewed without special equipment, and used to make 35mm slides. They can also be used without dimming the lights in the classroom.

Disadvantages

Many people try to put too much information on a transparency. When this occurs, the effect of this medium is diminished and, at times, the medium becomes counter-productive. As with much of the newer technology, the use of overhead transparencies is dependent on the quality of the projector. Focusing can be a problem of space and distance from a screen. Projector bulbs can blow out at inconvenient times, with a replacement often not readily available.

Recommendations

Overhead transparencies are one of the simplest and most widely used tools to enhance classroom learning. They assist students in following a lecture. Their use for presenting a chart, diagram, or other graphic illustration has made them as indispensable as the chalkboard.

2. 35 mm (2" x 2") SLIDES

Slide sets are heavily used in art appreciation courses and in geography courses where no amount of oral or written description can substitute for a photograph of, for example, a painting or a mountain range. For a series of still pictures, especially in color, a set of 35mm slides has many advantages. This relatively simple medium requires a projector and a screen. Like the overhead projector, a blank, smooth white wall can substitute for the screen. However, bulbs in slide projectors seem to burn out more readily than in overhead projectors and the wise professor has a back-up at hand. Commercial slide sets often have a synchronized audiotape to accompany each slide. Again, the media center should be consulted about available slides and slide sets.

How

Black and white slides can be made of any material that might be made into transparencies. A few slides can be carried around easily and hand-fed into the projector. Slides are more durable than transparencies and the professor may wish to make slides of frequently used illustrations, tables, and graphs.

Previewing the slide set is necessary to check that all the slides are in the correct position and that none are upside down or sideways! Timing the presentation is also important. Checking the synchronization, if any, is also necessary.

Most slide projectors today have a remote control for changing slides and for focusing. The remote control enables the professor to talk to the class from the front of the room. The use of a pointer often helps to indicate a particular aspect of a slide in a set that the professor is changing manually.

Advantages

When a picture is worth a thousand words, 35mm slides are an indispensable tool. Unless the slides are an audio-synchronized presentation, the professor can determine the pace at which they are shown, spending time commenting on an important slide and going more swiftly through less important ones.

Disadvantages

Although black and white slides can be shown in ambient light, colored slides are best projected in a darkened room. This environment is difficult for students wishing to take notes. Note taking is also more difficult when the student needs to concentrate on looking up at the slide while needing to look down to write.

Various projectors have different arrangements for the slides. Changing slides from a stacking tray to carousel can be time consuming and can often result in a slide being upside down or sideways. After changing from one slide container to another, the slide set should be previewed.

Recommendations

Using 35mm slides is useful, especially when colored pictures are needed as part of a course. They do require a projector in working order, a screen, and a room that can be darkened. Slides are very useful for illustration, especially in subject areas such as geography and art appreciation where verbal description cannot convey adequate information about course concepts and topics.

3. OPAQUE PROJECTIONS

The opaque projector is a large and clumsy piece of equipment, seldom very satisfactory to use. However, when the course objectives are best achieved by presenting a page from a book or a picture for which no slide is available, the opaque projector is a useful machine. Care must be taken, however, that the page or picture is not left in the projector for more than two or three minutes. The projector emits enough heat to burn the page or picture. When possible, try another projection medium.

4. MOTION PICTURE FILMS AND VIDEOTAPES

The easy-to-use and produce videotape cassette is rapidly replacing the more difficult motion picture film in many college and university classroom situations. Many media centers are converting motion picture films to videocassette form. The videocassettes are easy to store and less subject to mishandling by students and professors.

Films and videotapes are available for many subjects and can be used for many purposes in a classroom. They are very useful for demonstrating the actions and techniques required for certain skills. They are heavily used in professional areas. Films can illustrate motion and habitat more effectively than any other common, easily available medium. Films can illustrate social history, language, and culture. They are considered an art form as well as an educational medium.

How

Films and videotapes are usually available in a college or university media collection. They can also be rented from a commercial source using library or departmental funds; however, arrangements for film rental must usually be made months in advance of the anticipated date for use. Also, arrangements must be made with the media center to schedule both the film and a suitable (and reliable) projector in the classroom. All films and videotapes must be previewed before use. The class must be prepared for the content of the film and alerted to important aspects to look for. The film should be discussed both before and after the class sees it.

Advantages

The cassette can be more easily stopped at a particular point or slowed down for closer viewing of a particulate motion of interest. In fact, in any area where motion is an important element of the pictorial record, the videocassette is the teaching tool of choice. A video recording can be done in class or brought to class when details of particular segments need to be reviewed for accuracy of observation or analysis.

A particular advantage of the video is the ability of the student to use it outside the classroom to reinforce and master classroom instruction. The student can watch a videotape on his or her own once a technique has been explained in class. Working with the tape, the student can practice the technique over and over in a laboratory situation until it is mastered.

Disadvantages

Previewing a film or video is vital to having it achieve the professor's objectives. Equipment in good condition is also essential.

Recommendations

The videocassette, rapidly replacing the motion picture on a reel, is a particularly useful tool for teaching skills and techniques, for showing action, and for illustrating habitat and culture. The video can be made available to the student for ready reference during the learning process, not only in the laboratory but also in the dormitory and the home since the videocassette player has become such a widely purchased piece of household equipment.

5. AUDIOTAPES AND RECORDS

Audio technology is especially useful in music and in language courses as well as in any course where the professor would like the class to hear a particular personality speak in his or her own voice. For instance, the Fireside Chats of Franklin Roosevelt are far more interesting on record or audiotape in his own voice than they are when read in a book. Audiotapes and records are particularly useful in speech-related courses.

How

This learning medium is relatively simple, involving only an aural medium such as a 33rpm recording, a compact disk, or an audiotape, usually in a plastic cassette. Whichever medium is selected, a compatible player and/or recording device will also be required.

Advantages

As a motivational method, audiotapes with the recorded voice of a famous personality are very useful. In language courses, students can compare their language facility and accent with that of a native speaker who they are trying to emulate. In music, neither the written word nor a photograph can substitute for a stereophonically recorded audiotape. The compact disk (CD) is rapidly replacing the 33rpm record for classroom listening. The audiocassette is also popular.

Disadvantages

Students today have become very proficient at utilizing two incoming information channels at the same time. Unless the auditory medium is used in conjunction with another activity (such as taking notes or watching a set of slides or a film), the student may not absorb as much information from this medium as the professor would expect. For the same reason, an audio presentation should generally be no longer than 5-10 minutes at a time.

Recommendations

Audio tapes and records should be used by themselves only when the objectives of a particular lesson focus on the human voice or on sound itself. The quality of the sound recorded should be carefully checked before using a particular recording in class since sound quality can often be poor.

6. TELEVISION TECHNOLOGY

The use of television technology for demonstration was discussed earlier in this chapter in #14 under Methods of Presenting Course Content. Television can be used for classroom presentation at remote sites on campuses and at greater distances. Entire courses have long been given by television. Preparation and production for such use is complex and not discussed here. Programs and pieces of programs can be obtained for video use in the classroom. Large television monitors should be hooked up so that programs or projections from a computer monitor can be seen by the entire class.

7. COMPUTER-ASSISTED COURSEWARE

Computer-assisted courseware is a developing area of learning media. Its impact on the curriculum is difficult to measure; however, its use is becoming more pervasive. Computers are increasingly used in classroom teaching. They are used in writing classes to illustrate how to develop a critical outline. In drama classes, visual editors can show the development of stage plays. In biology, programs are available to illustrate anatomy, providing close-ups and detail as needed. For chemistry, molecular editors can be used to show molecular structure, synthesis, and reactions. The sciences and mathematics (including statistics) have long used computer courseware as a teaching tool. However, more courseware is now being developed and tested in the social sciences as well as in the arts and humanities.

Much courseware is being developed as games and as simulations to actively involve students in the learning process. Games and simulations enable immediate feedback. A technique called "hypertext" explores the use of the computer in conjunction with other media to encourage and enable students to control a body of information to meet their needs and interests. The use of courseware should be carefully evaluated for quality of content, ease of use, and relevance to course objectives before incorporating a particular package into the course design.

Professors in many subject disciplines will wish to investigate computer-assisted courseware for teaching. Development of courseware packages, however, is so time consuming that the nonspecialist will benefit from acquiring existing packages. However, some professors, with the assistance of instructional support personnel, may wish to undertake a team effort to develop a customized courseware package for a specific classroom purpose. Instructional support departments may be helpful in this effort.

•••••••••••••••••••••••

These techniques are intended to point out various ways of presenting in the classroom. There are, of course, many others. Some of these are specific to certain disciplines. Some require specialized skills and interests on the part of the professor. The learning manager will devise techniques of her own. This is part of the teaching art.

Chapter **6**

LABORATORY LEARNING

In laboratories students work directly with materials and equipment in a tutorial relationship with instructors. The division of a course into classroom study, out-of-class learning, and laboratory is artificial. Laboratories traditionally have been *places* of work. Yet it has always been possible to take a specimen or microscope home for study or to conduct an experiment in the field. With computers and telecommunications, scholars in many fields are less tied to a specific place of work. Data may be recorded in one place and transmitted to another for examination and study, either in real time or at some subsequent time. Data may be accessed remotely and downloaded to a personal computer or transmitted by facsimile.

Therefore, for the purposes of this book, laboratory learning is defined more loosely as *using equipment and material* to do the work of a specific discipline. The scholarly labor is investigative work. The objective is to find out—or, in lower-level courses, to learn how to find out—in the particular area of knowledge. The process of "finding out," especially in the fine arts and some technological areas, may include the development of a particular skill. Instead of listening to information about the subject or discussing the subject in the classroom, instead of reading about the subject or reviewing what others have said, the student directly investigates the subject itself. Naturally, such an artificial distinction leads to all kinds of overlap and inconsistencies. For example, practice in speaking a language takes place in a language class. Nevertheless, the professor may wish to distinguish between the "doing" and the "talking about" in course planning. Otherwise, to use an extreme example, a student of chemistry could learn to discuss and write about chemistry, but would have no experience in working with chemicals.

Even in the field of literature, where library work has been the traditional "laboratory" experience, current equipment enables students to do more than read literature and critiques of literature. Computers can be used for textual analysis. Various kinds of content analysis, comparison of facsimile editions, and the use of syntax analyzers are now possible.

From this point of view, laboratory work may be designed for a much broader array of subject areas than has been traditional by making available the materials and equipment for students to investigate the subject matter of the field. The laboratory experience emphasizes participatory learning by having the student work individually or in small groups. Direct involvement, actually working with a subject, has been known for years as the most effective way to learn. Although laboratory experience may not enable the student to acquire subject-related experience at a professional level, the laboratory experience clearly will lead to a greater understanding of the subject and of professional expectations in the field.

Laboratory instruction, whether or not it transpires in places specifically called laboratories, is taught with the help of an instructor or lab assistant. The instructor is available to work with the student in a tutorial mode, providing explanations, encouragement, and immediate feedback.

Brown and Atkins identify the goals of laboratory instruction as follows (p 91):

"1) Teaching manual and observational skills relevant to the subject

2) Improving understanding of methods of scientific enquiry

3) Developing problem-solving skills

4) Nurturing professional attitudes."

In reviewing the literature comparing lecture methods, discussion methods, and laboratory training, Brown and Atkins (p 11) state: "Practical skills are obviously taught more effectively in laboratories." Beard and Hartley (p 196) surveyed the goals of professors using laboratory methods in various institutions. They list the following goals:

1) To become critically aware

2) To stimulate and maintain interests

3) To teach how to handle data as the basis for teaching report writing and keeping a laboratory notebook

4) To encourage informal interaction between staff and individual students

5) To illustrate lecture material

6) To train in experimental design

7) To teach theory not covered by lectures
8) To develop manipulative skills.

Laboratory experiences should be considered for a wide variety of courses in addition to the traditional laboratory sciences. The following sections deal with natural and physical science laboratories, social and behavioral science laboratories, fine arts and humanities, personalized systems of instruction, alternative laboratory methods, and field work.

NATURAL AND PHYSICAL SCIENCE LABORATORIES

Laboratories for the natural and physical sciences are usually designed to provide the student with the opportunity to observe phenomena not readily observed in the classroom and/or learn particular techniques. Laboratories are also designed to teach students to record and analyze data by having them write up their observations and analyses in a scientific manner.

The professor should recognize that most undergraduate laboratory experiences are somewhat artificial in the sense that the results of a structured laboratory session are already known. Therefore, for most undergraduates, the laboratory experience will rarely convey the excitement of discovering new knowledge, the impetus of curiosity, the impulse to know, the drive to explore. However, the laboratory is an excellent place to experiment and to gain experience with a new subject. The laboratory is a place where the student can learn something he or she could not do before.

How

The professor must become acquainted with the subject-related science laboratories available for use by his classes. This acquaintance involves learning the layout of the lab, the quantity and condition of equipment and materials. An acquaintance with the budget for materials and supplies is essential, as is a familiarity with the ordering and receiving processes (especially the lead time required for ordering and receiving new or replacement materials and supplies). The professor should know which other faculty members will be sharing the lab as well as the number, availability and qualifications of laboratory assistants.

Each laboratory exercise should be designed to provide the student with the opportunity to learn a technique, make an observation, or become directly involved in a process that cannot be carried out in the classroom. The laboratory experiments should be related to major course goals instead of incidental objectives. Avoid experiments that have only historical interest. Emphasize the relationship between the laboratory work and the concepts being learned in class. Integrate the sequence of the lab experiments with the sequence of classroom topics.

Prepare a lab manual for student use well in advance of each scheduled laboratory session. The lab manual should describe the experiment, including how to set up any apparatus and/or specimens. A step-by-step procedure for performing the experiment must be included. Clearly and precisely describe what and how to observe, count, or measure. Specify what and how to record in a lab notebook and specify the format for any lab report to be handed in.

General instructions given in the lab itself should be very brief in order to enable the student to spend the maximum time in the lab period working on his or her own, with a lab partner, or in a small group. A demonstration of a particular technique or process should be given when required. Be available to assist students and to answer questions.

Laboratory sections or discussion groups are frequently part of the design of courses with regular laboratories. Sections provide an opportunity to discuss the relationship of laboratory work to in-class work and assignments. They also provide an opportunity for review and synthesis. Discussion sections can also be used for demonstration, assistance with calculations, informal instruction and explanation, as well as introduction to the next session of laboratory work. Discussion sections are frequently conducted by laboratory assistants. In courses without regularly scheduled discussion sections, the above should be covered in class.

Advantages

• Problem-solving and investigative skills can be taught and nurtured in a professional atmosphere.

• Supervision permits individualized instruction, guidance, encouragement, and feedback.

• Student learns by doing, especially subject-related techniques, procedures, and the scientific method.

• Practical skills training may be helpful for future employment.

• Student learns how to detect errors in his or her own work, the time involved in correcting careless or avoidable errors, and how to work through difficulties encountered in a "real" problem.

Disadvantages

- Standard experiments do not have the thrill of true investigative work, of discovering new knowledge.
- Student may be discouraged from being creative in order to accomplish the structured objectives of the lab.
- Student may learn only "cookbook" techniques and processes.

Conclusions

The laboratory is the only way to learn some things, the best way to learn others. It is the best way to learn practical skills. It individualizes and personalizes instruction. At best, it is the training ground for the scientists of the future.

SOCIAL AND BEHAVIORAL SCIENCE LABORATORIES

In the social and behavioral science lab, the professor provides the opportunity for students to learn by actually applying the constructs and models of the various social and behavioral science disciplines. Where the natural and physical sciences have a scheduled laboratory period as part of the course, the social sciences may have laboratory periods scheduled off-campus as part of a term project or included in classroom instruction. Students learn by testing the various constructs and models based on limited amounts of data they have collected. The students can learn the techniques and methods of data collection, manipulation, analysis, and simulation. Sometimes students participate in collecting data for an ongoing study. The professor may also design experiments using large databases such as census data, stock market data and the like. Simulations are especially useful, and there are many available.

Laboratory-related experiences in the social sciences may include learning how to construct and validate a questionnaire, how to select and administer standardized tests measuring various personal or social attributes, how and when to apply various research designs (especially observational and survey research designs), how to use a protocol, etc.

How

Decide on lab goals and objectives, specifically how the lab sessions will supplement and complement classroom material. Find the appropriate data sets and derive subsets as needed. Before proceeding, determine the budget available for the laboratory work, including the budget for computer time. Design experiments that will illustrate major constructs, avoiding trivial or merely do-able experiences. Design a protocol for any data collection project, specifying reporting requirements and evaluative techniques. The use of existing data sets such as census figures, election returns, stock market figures, etc., enables the professor to provide experience with real data. Make use of the computer lab and the various statistical packages available to save time and increase accuracy in data analysis.

Prepare the students, either in the classroom or at the beginning of the laboratory session. Introduce the experiment, emphasizing the procedures that are to be used. Be available during the lab session for individualized instruction. Integrate the experiment with classroom work and outside readings either in class or in laboratory discussion.

Advantages

• The student learns to apply theoretical constructs and models, and to understand the numerous variables which have to be considered in social science research.

• Student learns to practice accepted methodology and to work with data.

• Student learns to apply appropriate statistical tests to data to determine levels of confidence in the analytical results.

• Student learns to work with a team, especially when the lab experience involves a survey.

• Student learns job-related skills and techniques.

Disadvantages

• Because of the lack of standard experimental exercises, the design effort is time-consuming.

• Students may be frightened of data, statistical manipulation, or use of equipment.

• Designing exercises to illustrate more than a small number of principles is very difficult.

Note: When using human subjects, determine the school policy; adhere to federal policies and the ethical stance of the discipline. Experiments with human subjects provide an excellent opportunity for class discussion of ethical issues.

Conclusions

Laboratories are a significant way of making theoretical constructs real in the social sciences. They provide practical skills and an important opportunity for participative learning. Like all laboratories, they individualize learning in a feedback environment. They can be used to advantage in many social science courses.

FINE ARTS AND HUMANITIES LABORATORIES

The fine arts and humanities, like some social sciences, do not use a laboratory in the generally accepted sense of the word. However, many areas of the fine arts and performing arts utilize the studio to teach techniques and procedures in a manner similar to the laboratories previously described in this chapter. The so-called language laboratory is often a studio for honing pronunciation and inflection in a foreign language and being exposed to aspects of culture using film and, increasingly, interactive video.

As text and pictures become increasingly available in digitized form using the computer, linguists, historians, and literary scholars are able to analyze the materials in their disciplines in new ways. Indeed, the impact of the computer on historical scholarship has resulted in the development of a new subfield called cliometrics, in honor of Clio, the muse of history. Music, as a research subject, has also felt the impact of the computer and other electronic technology in the form of the synthesizer, of digital editing of orchestral recordings, etc. The development of optical techniques for recording and storing sound, pictures, and data will simply add to this impact on scholarship and research in the fine arts and humanities.

The computer is clearly a tool for innovative teaching in the fine arts and humanities. Computer art is becoming recognized as a new medium requiring technique and creativity. Inexpensive synthesizers which may be hooked up to computers and speakers are revolutionizing musical composition. The wide availability of VCRs has placed the study of film material within easy reach. Concordances are available in computer-readable form for a wide array of textual material. Computer programs for various types of textual analysis have been available for years. Facsimiles of writers' notes, manuscripts, editions and the like are available on microform.

Compact discs with video are beginning to integrate text, still pictures, and graphics for study without expensive computer connect-time. An encyclopedia is already available in this form. The power of this new medium is illustrated by the Domesday Project. To use this medium, the student sits at a compact disc terminal with a keyboard and a "mouse." The student might start in a museum where it is possible to "walk" around by moving the mouse, zoom in on pictures, go around sculptures and view them from behind, then proceed into other rooms as desired. When interest is piqued, text can be obtained about the artist by the mere press of a button. When bored, the student can wander (on screen) out onto the street of the town. If interested, a press of a button will obtain text about the history of the town or graphic data about industry, demography and the like. The student can also wander into a home to see what it looks like. The Domesday Project is but one illustration of the kind of material being developed by museums and others. This material has the potential to open a whole new world and a whole new way of studying the humanities. Technology offers incredible opportunities to bring scholarly material to the student for study.

The following suggestions for implementing laboratories in the humanities involve making material (and perhaps equipment) available to the student for study individually or in small groups, under the professor's supervision for guidance, encouragement, and feedback.

How

First, decide what the students are to learn to do. Next, obtain the material to be worked on and arrange appropriate space—frequently, study rooms in the library can be used. Then design the exercises, including a formal set of instructions. Students may be asked to take notes. The notes may be integrated with an outside written assignment.

Advantages

- In the laboratory the professor has the opportunity to work with students in the tutorial mode when introducing difficult and unfamiliar material and processes as well as methods of analysis.
- Students can be more easily introduced to the tools of modern scholarship in the laboratory environment than in the classroom.

Disadvantages

- In many areas of the humanities the professor may be unfamiliar with the use of laboratory instruction.
- The professor may find the initial design effort difficult.

Conclusion

Humanities laboratories provide an opportunity for innovative teaching. Instruction in advanced methods of scholarship can be individualized so that the professor serves as tutor.

MASTERY LEARNING
AND PERSONALIZED PROGRAMS
OF INSTRUCTION

Mastery learning comes out of the behavioral tradition in psychology. It is based on the idea that the rate of learning can be influenced by reinforcement. In mastery learning, as described by Guskey, the student is given frequent tests. The tests are prescriptive; that is, they are administered to diagnose what the student has learned and what specific activities are needed to achieve mastery (p 86). The results of the tests fulfill the criteria determined by Guskey for effective teachers to enhance individual student development; i.e., they are immediate, specific, and prescriptive (p 36, 60). Mastery course design is group-oriented, the pace being controlled by the professor. Learning 80-90 percent of the material is considered mastery (pp 47-60). Disciplines in which mastery has been used include biology, counseling, English composition, history, mathematics, nursing, psychology, reading, and Spanish (p 56).

In contrast to instruction where the pace of the learning is under the control of the professor, a great deal of interest has been generated in student-paced individual learning. Like mastery learning, these methods are based on modularized, sequential learning units with frequent testing and feedback. Some of the content material is formatted in text or workbooks such as a programmed textbook. Other content material uses instructional technology ranging from audio-tutorial material and machines for programmed instruction to computer-based instruction. Starting in the 1960s a lot of useful material was developed with special machines. Computer-assisted-instruction (CAI) material is, in general, still not as useful as the best of other print or technology-based material.

CAI differs from computer-aided learning. The latter is not based on behavioral principles. That is, computer-aided learning is not dependent on the use of specific testing and reinforcement at each step. In CAI, the modularized learning units, frequently called frames, are followed by an objective test of recall. As a result of the performance on the test, the student either advances to the next sequence or is given further material and explanation and is tested again. Constructing valid, reliable material for this type of learning is extremely time consuming. The learning manager who wishes to use this method should consult the *APLET Yearbook of Educational and Instructional Technology* (APLET).

The student-paced individual learning method that has received the most attention is called Personalized Systems of Instruction (PSI) or Keller Plan. As described by Guskey (p 53):

> It is essentially an extension of "programmed instruction" that includes a personal/social element. That is, in a PSI class, the feedback to students about the adequacy or inadequacy of their learning is provided by people—usually student proctors—rather than by a computer terminal or designed set of instructional materials. Students typically work at their own pace and move on to new material only after they have demonstrated perfect mastery of each unit. In addition, students may retake mastery tests at the end of each unit any number of times without penalty. Those who do not pass the mastery test repeat the original instructional unit and retake the test whenever they believe they are prepared.
>
> The teacher's role in a PSI class is primarily to give individual assistance as needed. Occasional class presentations are seen as vehicles of motivation rather than as sources of critical information. Therefore, carefully designed, self-instructional materials are essential to a successful PSI program.

Individualized learning methods characterized by the use of technology, modularized instruction, frequent tests, and student activity with less formal presentation by the professor have been subjected to a great deal of research, which is reviewed by Dunkin & Barnes. In studies of student achievement and satisfaction, innovative methods show a small superiority in achievement, but not satisfaction, with the exception of Personalized Systems of Instruction (PSI), which are often better on both. PSI is more effective in mathematics, engineering, and psychology than in the physical sciences, life sciences, or other social sciences. The significant aspects of PSI are "mastery, frequent quizzes, immediate feedback and review units, but not proctor tutoring, self-pacing, explicit objectives, and occasional lectures."

These research results will encourage those who believe that mastery and individually-paced learning methods are not the be-all and end-all. The results may serve to dampen the enthusiasm of those who believe otherwise. The use of review units is standard practice in most course design. The advantages of immediate feedback are well known, although often honored in the breach. Frequent quizzes are also appropriate to many course designs, especially where learning is incremental and understanding of one unit is dependent on a thorough grounding in the preceding units. When the student does well, learning and retention are enhanced. Finally, mastery is an appropriate goal and evaluative criterion for any course with performance objectives, whether the goal is called mastery or not.

Mastery learning, however, is not appropriate to all course goals. Much cognitive learning is non-specific and difficult to assess objectively. Changes in student values are notoriously difficult to assess. Learning also derives from performance or participatory learning. For example, a goal might be a feeling for what the potential errors (and their likelihood) are in an investigative technique. While some errors can be specified, only actual experience with the technique would achieve this goal. The ability to set such goals is, indeed, a rationale for laboratory experience.

ALTERNATIVE LABORATORY METHODS

There are many alternatives to standard laboratory methods. Among those listed by Brown and Atkins are the following:
• Students interpret the data which are provided.
• Students note, calculate, and interpret the results of a video of the experiment.
• Students only do the part of the experiment that can be done quickly, working with prepared materials for the slow part.
• Computer-assisted learning can be used to provide simulations of phenomena that could not be studied directly because of cost or complexity (pp 101-102).

FIELD STUDIES

Field studies have long been used in certain subjects. In the 1970s, in response to students' cries for "relevance," the use of field studies increased. The *Guide to Effective Teaching* reports field work courses designed around interviewing, intergenerational experience, classrooms in industry, exploring forgotten urban spaces, museums, study abroad, and behavior therapy.

Field studies are a significant aspect of participatory learning. They can be used either as a small part or a significant part of a wide range of courses. As always, field studies need to be an integral part of the course design. The specific methods differ widely. In general, the student needs adequate background to take advantage of the experience. The student needs to know what to do, and there should be frequent contact with the professor for mentoring. Frequently, the student meets with other students and the professor, either in the field or back in the classroom, to discuss the experience.

•••••••••••••••••

In summary, student laboratory experience as defined here involves: (1) working with the subject matter of the field; (2) having specific procedural instructions (as in a lab manual); and (3) being supervised by the professor or by assistants for guidance, feedback, and mentoring. For the professor, managing laboratory learning includes: (1) defining specific goals; (2) making materials available for study; (3) developing the procedures for students to use; and (4) integrating the laboratory with the rest of the course experience.

One thing that distinguishes the laboratory experience from outside assignments is mentoring. The professor and/or the laboratory assistants (proctors, in the case of PSI) are available during the session to assist, explain, and encourage the student during the learning process. Rather than learning *about* theory, laboratories give students an opportunity to derive theory and to apply theory to data to learn what happens. If the student does not have an interest in pursuing scholarly investigation (and most do not), he or she still is better prepared as the result of laboratory experience to evaluate scholarly investigation as an educated citizen.

Chapter 7

COURSE ASSIGNMENTS

Assignments done outside of specified class or laboratory time usually constitute a major part of the student's work during a course. Assignments constructed with particular learning objectives in mind are an important part of the course design effort. Although the student's attitude may affect learning, outside assignments can generate enthusiasm and interest for classroom activities. Outside assignments generally provide more learning for the student than any test or examination.

Assignments represent a major method of attaining the goals and objectives of the course by complementing and enhancing the classroom and laboratory learning. The learning manager who primarily lectures in class may wish to encourage discussion and problem-solving with assignments; indeed, discussion sections for large classes serve just this purpose. The class that is primarily discussion oriented may depend upon assignments to gather the information needed for discussion. Assignments to visit museums, take field trips, make on-site observations, and conduct interviews and surveys may supplement, extend, and even serve in place of a laboratory.

Students can be encouraged to do many things as a result of clearly structured, goal-oriented assignments. By the same token, students need to believe they will benefit from the assignments. Claims of "make-work" assignments often happen because the students do not see how assignments will benefit them.

DESIGNING ASSIGNMENTS

Assignments are obviously intended to help the students learn the material; they are most successful when they are designed with specific goals in mind. The orientation of the course will, in large measure, determine the type of assignment the professor will design. Assignments have the following different orientations that should be considered in their design:

• **Preparation for class**. These are assignments that the students need to complete before attending class. This type of assignment includes reading specified materials and preparing to respond to particular questions by developing arguments and preparing to discuss observations or materials that the student has examined.

• **Follow-up and extension of material presented in class**. These assignments include reviewing readings discussed in class, practicing solving problems using methods introduced in class, thinking and reviewing the implications of material presented in class and discussing such material with others.

• **Problem solving**. Problem solving assignments range from homework in mathematics and statistics courses to term papers and projects. These assignments can be used to help students learn particular techniques in a particular field. They can also be used to develop creative and critical thinking in analyzing a problem, then in synthesizing classroom learning and outside materials to solve the problem.

• **Applying knowledge to produce a product**. These assignments include written exercises, short essays, summarizations of readings, and creations of models or designs. Students usually enjoy application assignments. However, these assignments should be designed so that they challenge the brilliant student and at the same time do not overwhelm the less-capable student. Designing application assignments to suit the learning capacity of a range of student abilities is a challenge for even the most skillful professor.

• **Review of class material**. These assignments involve organizing the work presented in class, the supplementary materials, and the assignments completed in preparation for quizzes, tests, and examinations. Students usually benefit from going over subject content when preparing for a test or exam. Considering course goals and objectives helps to focus reviews.

In addition to considering the orientation of the course when designing assignments, the following questions may also be helpful:

- Given this law, rule, model, etc. explained in class, how can it be applied to real life or simulated situations?

- Given this way of thinking about trends, what trends can be predicted from the things learned so far in this course?

- Given the principles of analysis or design learned in this course, how can they be applied to one or more of the following situations?

- Given these data, how can they be evaluated?

- Given this discussion question, what information is needed to prepare for a debate, a panel discussion, an essay?

In sum, the purpose of assignments is to complement and enhance other work for the course. The design of assignments is an important part of the learning manager's planning effort.

STRUCTURING OUT-OF-CLASS ASSIGNMENTS

In general, the less-mature student requires more structure for outside assignments than the more mature and sophisticated student. However, the assignments should be so structured that the student takes the time to think critically about both the assignment and the material with which he or she is working. Mature reflection is one of the goals of scholarship, and the professor should try to foster critical thinking and creativity. But at the same time, the professor must consider the diversity of student learning styles. All students complain about "busywork," yet they are equally frightened by being left to flounder without sufficient direction to complete an assignment that will satisfy the professor and result in a good grade. Outside assignments, especially term papers and projects, usually constitute a significant percentage of a student's final grade for the course as well as a major portion of his or her learning from the course.

Key considerations in structuring out-of-class assignments include:

- **Relationship to goals and objectives**. Any assignment not related to goals and objectives is busywork.

- **Helping students learn how to learn in a particular field of knowledge**. Different subject areas require different techniques for analysis, synthesis, and problem-solving. The professor is responsible for instructing students in these techniques. For example, successful design of a computer program requires a structured, modularized approach. Students need to learn this approach before attempting a significant programming assignment.

- **Making material available to facilitate learning**. The student who has to spend hours looking for material will have less time to use the material for learning. Unless the assignment objective is the searching process, the professor will enable the student to be more productive by providing easy access to the materials necessary for learning. In reading assignments, for example, the professor will often place reading materials on the reserve shelf in the library.

- **Introducing the most important materials**. For term papers, the professor might mention authors key to the assignment. For initial programming courses, the professor might introduce the students to the hardware, the operating system, and key aspects of the software required to solve a programming problem.
- **Focusing learning**. Some courses, especially in a professional studies area, use classroom time for teaching basic concepts. Outside assignments designed to apply these concepts enable the student to see the purpose of the classroom learning.

HOW MUCH TO EXPECT

Many college freshmen have graduated from high school doing little homework. The fact that they may have been among the brightest students in their high school class may have contributed to their ability to learn high school material while doing little or no homework.

The traditional expectation for undergraduate learning is three hours spent working on course-related assignments for every hour spent in the classroom. Students need to become aware of this expectation, especially since most learning in college is accomplished outside the classroom. Therefore, most students who put off working on a course until the last few weeks of the term cannot expect to learn as much or to do as well in the course as students who work more steadily throughout the term.

One way of insuring that students, especially freshmen, will learn to work more steadily throughout the term is to design progress-report type assignments that will provide feedback to the professor on the quantity and quality of the student's work. Such feedback assignments also enable the professor to detect and assist students having difficulties with the work. Each student should learn how to achieve his or her own goals and at the same time satisfy the requirements for the course.

The professor teaching graduate students should assume that they know how to find their own material for learning. Graduate students should also need much less guidance about the level and quality of work expected. In most graduate courses, outside assignments, which indicate the ability of the student to do independent work, are a critical component of the course as well as of the graduate program itself. Expectations for upper-level undergraduates range between those for first-year students and those for graduate students.

TYPES OF ASSIGNMENTS

The construction of relevant, imaginative assignments requires a lot of time. However, many "tried and true" assignments continue to be used because they have been found effective in managing learning. Assignments will differ according to the subject area and the level of both the course and the student. The following are commonly used types of assignments.

• **Readings**. Most courses have a significant number of reading assignments. They range from a chapter in a textbook for some intensive courses, especially in the sciences and mathematics, to a whole novel in a literature class. Readings may be assigned to prepare for class or to supplement classroom presentation or both. Frequently other readings are suggested. Supplementary readings may be listed on the course syllabus. Often different students in a class are pursuing different topics as outside reading. Usually, a great deal of reading is done in preparation for writing papers. Readings may stimulate students to pursue individual interests on their own.

In making reading assignments it is important that the amount of reading not appear overwhelming. For this reason, the suggested reading list should be short and the supplementary one somewhat longer. The challenge in devising reading assignments is to select items that will stimulate interest and capture the imagination of the students.

• **Writing**. Writing assignments are appropriate for many courses. There are a variety that are commonly used. With the current emphasis on the value of communication skills, many colleges have instituted a concept called Writing-Across-the-Curriculum where writing assignments are an important complement to course content and are well-integrated in the course design.

Essays—Essays represent the students' thinking about a specific topic that was encountered in class or outside work. Essays may be as short as two hand-written pages. They may represent students' attempts to analyze or synthesize ideas. They may also represent students' thoughts on a particular topic. Sometimes it is effective to assign such essay writing to be done during the class period.

Journals or Logs—A journal or log of activities or thoughts related to a particular topic in the course or to the course itself can be used to integrate classroom activities, readings, and other experiences. They help the student track problems to be overcome and progress in learning the course material.

Abstracts and Annotations—It is useful for students to learn how to write informative and descriptive abstracts of articles. Abstracts are

101

frequently required to accompany journal publication or to accompany submissions in response to calls for papers. Such assignments are useful for learning to write succinctly.

Book Reviews—Book reviews are appropriate in literature courses. They are preferable to book reports. An ideal model for a book review or critique is *The New York Review of Books.*

Reports—Reports may be descriptive and/or evaluative. Assignments of reports of activities such as field observations or museum visits should be structured so that the student is clear about the type and format. Laboratory reports are a common, highly structured report form. Memo writing is a brief report form increasingly used as an assignment in order to monitor student progress on a major project.

Short Papers—A number of short papers provide the student an opportunity to improve his or her writing skills during the course and complete written work across the semester rather than having it all due at the end. This distribution across the semester also provides the student the opportunity to learn from and react to the professor's guidance and evaluation of the papers.

Literature Reviews—Reviews are a way of bringing together the essence of articles and books read. Such reviews may be critical or noncritical.

Creative Writing—Creative writing is, naturally, used in courses on creative writing. Not all students take such courses. Encouraging creativity and original thinking in students is important. Assignments requiring creativity should be considered for many courses.

Term Papers—Term papers are among the most common assignments, especially in upper-level courses. Eble (pp 132-137) argues cogently against the ubiquitous use of term papers. When term papers are used, the purpose of the assignment should be very clear to the student. The instructions for the term paper should always be in writing and the evaluative criteria specified. (See the suggestions in the Evaluation chapter on evaluating term papers.) Breaking term-paper assignments into blocks that can be separately monitored and evaluated may be helpful. Thus, topic choice, bibliography, literature review, outline, rough draft, second draft, and final paper can be assigned sequentially. Eble suggests that in designing term papers, the professor should differentiate between "looking it up," "thinking about it," and "expressing it" (Eble, pp 136-137).

• **Drill and Practice**. Practice exercises are important when facts need to be internalized. Exercises are frequently used in introductory language classes for practice on vocabulary, verb forms, and translation. They may be helpful for development of terminology in many subjects, such as organic chemistry; indeed, exercises are helpful in any area in which recall is necessary.

Textbooks are often sources of such exercises. The professor may wish to use selected exercises from a number of texts not used in the courses. The textbook used for the courses may have exercises that can be assigned. Students learn more quickly when the answers are immediately available.

To facilitate the learning process, *programmed instruction* was developed in the 1950s for use either in book form or with special machines. By the 1970s computer applications were developed to do the same thing. This is called *computer-assisted instruction.* Both programmed instruction and computer-assisted instruction have been developed for whole courses, such as statistics and calculus.

• **Problem Sets**. The sciences and mathematics usually assign problem sets as an opportunity to work through problems similar to those presented in class. These problem sets help the students to retain learning acquired in the classroom. Short problems that clearly illustrate the points explained in class may be more effective than multi-step problems. Process should be emphasized over arithmetic. In problems for the computer, data manipulation should be preferred over data entry.

• **Observations, Interviews, Testing, Experiments**. *Observations* provide valuable support for classroom work and reading. Observation can be assigned to students in many subject disciplines. For instance, observations can be made in a museum for art, the field for geology or botany, a shopping mall for sociology, a playground for child development.

Interviews can be used for oral history and many of the social sciences. *Test administration* can be an assignment. Simple *experiments* can be conducted without laboratory support.

• **Films, videotapes, etc.** At times, depending on the availability of equipment and media, assignments can be made to view a particular film, videotape, filmstrip, etc. in the library. The assignment can then be discussed in class without spending valuable class time on the film or tape itself.

• **Computer-assisted Learning.** Computer-assisted learning problems occur mainly in the areas of design, decision-making (including decision support), and simulations. An example of a design problem is in stage setting: the student can build the set step by step, moving the components around until a satisfactory set is produced. An example of decision-making is to determine what the outcome would be if different decisions were made in response to the October Missile Crisis, and then determine the optimal decision. In simulations, either steps are provided and the student supplies the inputs or the student can play with the structure (i.e., the steps) and find out what happens. Programs are available in a range of difficulty; e.g., from learning introductory economics to learning advanced economic forecasting.

Computer-assisted learning programs are available in many disciplines and the professor will wish to determine which might be useful to supplement learning.

• **Cases.** Cases give an opportunity to try to apply theoretical learning. The professor may encounter appropriate cases in the media, in her consulting practices, or from other experiences. The literature of the subject being studied frequently contains cases that can be used.

• **Projects.** Like writing assignments, projects can be simple or complex and time-consuming. The complex, time-consuming projects are usually a considerable portion of the course work. The projects can range from creating a design or model to writing, implementing, and documenting a complex computer program. Students at some engineering schools must produce working models illustrating design principles learned as part of a course.

• **Group Work.** Eble points out that much real-life work, not to mention academic life, is conducted by committees (p 135). Students need to learn to work in groups. The learning manager will design assignments that encourage students to interact together about the subject matter of the course. One possibility is to have students take different aspects of a problem. They may also work together on a particular problem. In any case, student discussion of course work outside of class is to be encouraged.

• **Questions.** Preparation for answering questions is good review. Questions may be used to orient and review readings. They are useful to focus preparation for class discussion. They are also useful in preparing for tests and examinations. Many professors make previous examination questions available for review. Students can be asked to make up exam questions which are then discussed during a review period. Professors can give out the actual essay examination questions in advance to assist students in reviewing. Sometimes review questions are given at the end of chapters in textbooks and may be assigned.

SOURCES OF ASSIGNMENTS

Texts may be sources for problem sets and questions for discussion. The pedagogical literature contains many tested examples. Many fields have journals with such titles as "Journal of Education in ...." Assignments may be borrowed from colleagues, particularly colleagues at other schools. Practitioners and friends may also have good suggestions.

DUE DATES

The professor should stagger the due dates of course assignments, tests, and exams for two reasons. First, students need a reasonable length of time to work on an assignment. Also, despite admonitions and mandated progress reports, many students will still wait until the last minute to do the major part of the work. Since student learning is the professor's primary goal, attention has to be paid to this negative aspect of student behavior. Second, the professor cannot provide timely feedback to students about their efforts if all course assignments are due at the same time. Staggering due dates will benefit both student and professor.

● ● ● ● ● ● ● ● ● ● ● ● ● ● ●

More information on assignments can be found elsewhere in this book. Mentoring and monitoring assignments are discussed in Chapter 9. Evaluation of assignments is discussed in Chapter 10. Laboratory work is discussed in Chapter 6.

Meanwhile, Eble's comments provide a fitting conclusion:

> As to advice I might give, an unremitting attention to fashioning useful work for students and a distrust of routine assignments are places to begin. Defining assignments carefully and connecting them with clearly defined aims are of first importance. Borrowing ideas from others, exploring the pedagogical literature for ideas, and adapting such ideas to one's specific needs should be standard teaching practices. Trying out assignments on ourselves and getting students' views about the worth of an assignment are necessary correctives to a teacher's one-sided view. Making assignments is among the most difficult of a teacher's routine duties. We know the worth of what we ask the students to do, but, for students, almost any assignment may seem to be busy-work if they don't see what purpose it serves. (Eble, p 142).

Chapter **8**

MANAGING INDIVIDUAL LEARNING

Formal or informal interpersonal interaction can be one of the most rewarding scholarly experiences for both student and professor. Many professors feel that their students are their "scholarly heirs" and put effort analogous to preparing a course in "bringing on" their students. The professor's pride in watching a former student receive professional accolades surpasses that of any beaming grandparent.

The professor's objective in supervising individual learning is to give the student the skills to achieve professional success in the student's chosen area of endeavor. This objective is accomplished by mentoring, providing encouragement and guidance, and by enthusiastically recognizing the student's accomplishments. The opportunity to interact, on an informal basis, with an intellectually curious student, can be a joyful time for the professor. The same opportunity with the student lacking curiosity or motivation can cause the professor untold frustration.

Managing individual learning ranges from informally assisting the student to formally interacting with him or her for the duration of an independent study or during work on a thesis or dissertation. Individual learning at other sites such as co-op or practicum generally involves both a professor and another person. That person supervises the student's work daily and confers with the professor as needed and as required by the college.

UNDERGRADUATE INDEPENDENT STUDY

Many. undergraduate programs provide an independent study option for the student who wishes to pursue a research project not included in the courses offered in the curriculum. Independent study projects are awarded college credits, supervised by a faculty member, and evaluated and graded. In general, the independent study is agreed upon by student and supervising faculty. An informal performance contract is drawn up stating the purpose and design of the study and giving some time limits for its completion. At this point the student can register for the independent study as if he or she were registering for a course.

Independent study fulfills three needs:

1) It permits students to pursue, in depth, topics not dealt with in faculty-directed classrooms, laboratories, or studios;

2) It helps students to develop valuable research skills;

3) It enables students to test mastery of principles, methods, and materials with the mentoring guidance of a faculty member having expertise in the area of the independent study.

Independent study may well lead to the capacity for independent learning throughout life.

Institutional policy governing independent study varies from one college or university to another. The newly hired professor who is approached to supervise this form of student research is advised to consult the department chairman or college catalog about specific policy and procedures.

A professor should be wary about commitment to an independent study. This is especially true for a graduating senior who needs just one more course, not offered in the student's last term, to complete graduation requirements. The following questions should be considered:

• Does the student's academic performance to date indicate that the student is actually capable of independent research?

• What additional time commitment (generally unpaid) on the part of the professor will be required for adequate supervision of the independent study?

• Is the proposed study worthy of the number of credits the student wishes to earn for it?

• Is the study do-able in the time available, considering other aspects of the student's course load, possible employment, and other extra-curricular activities?

• Might the student succumb to the level-of-effort letdown known as "senioritis"?

• What would the student's reaction be to an unsatisfactory evaluation of the research, resulting in preventing him or her from graduating?

• Independent study substitution for a required course is a special case. Was the required course, for which the independent study will substitute, missed as a result of the student's own poor planning? Or is the student in this fix as a result of circumstances beyond his or her control?

Undergraduate independent studies are often most successful when undertaken during the junior year or during the first term of the senior year. The junior level and first term senior level student is usually sufficiently mature to work independently and does not have the pressures and activities of imminent graduation distracting the research effort.

The professor can also benefit from guiding the student in an independent study project. Such guidance may encourage a student to consider graduate school or to pursue a particular line of career-related study. This guidance has great psychological rewards for the professor and can lead to a mutually beneficial mentoring relationship. However, the professor who uses the student's research for his own professional advancement might well be accused of questionable ethics—the more so since this kind of student research frequently involves the "scut work" of data-gathering, with minimal student involvement in data analysis, report writing, or credit in the publication of research results.

INDIVIDUAL STUDENT RESEARCH

If the student is undertaking a first, small research project, the professor will need to monitor this effort carefully. The student working on a master's thesis or a doctoral dissertation needs special kinds of help, in part because of the mystique that may accompany the process. Thesis and dissertation advising is discussed in the next section.

The professor should know the standard texts on research methods for his subject field as well as general guides and indexes to published material in the field. The professor will also want to enlist the help of the institution's librarian to assist the student in finding information not in the library's own collection by searching online databases and by securing materials through inter-library loan.

Problem Selection

The professor can help the student select a problem of manageable size for the time involved. The professor might have a list of potential research topics or be able to suggest a particular topic to match the student's interests.

The following methods for problem selection may also prove useful:
- Replicate a previous study.
- Extend a study.
- Take a model from one field and apply it to another.
- Take a model from one field and use a model or analysis method from another field in a cross-disciplinary approach.
- Compare two or more data sets.
- Attack an old issue with new tools.
- Investigate an emergent issue.
- Follow suggestions for further research in an article or dissertation.

The student's initial interest in a problem should be followed with a quick literature review to determine whether the problem has been investigated already and whether the problem merits investigation. The literature review will help refine the problem selected and may be helpful in research design.

Literature Review

The student should already be familiar with the use of the library. The advanced student should be familiar with the major journals, reviewing sources (annual reviews, etc.), and abstracting and/or indexing services for the field.

The professor may assist by suggesting:
- Key article(s) in the specific subject for follow-up of predecessor articles (articles in a list of references) and subsequent or descendent articles (articles subsequently citing the key article listed in a citation index);
- The most relevant reviewing source, i.e., an annual review or yearbook, etc.
- The abstracting and/or indexing service most likely to include relevant material;
- Key words and/or subject categories to use in searching an abstracting and/or indexing service. *Note:* The student must understand that a negative search may mean that material is indexed under a term he or she has not thought of. The student should be careful about stopping the literature search too soon. This is especially important because the student must know whether the problem has been investigated. The professor is expected to be sufficiently familiar with the literature to recognize glaring omissions in the literature search and to suggest related areas and/or key words to pursue;

• Key researchers publishing in the subject field.

The student should already know the correct bibliographic citation format. If the college or university has a special format or standard, this should be given to the student before the literature search to save later rechecking and rewriting. The student should know how to take and organize notes about the literature, e.g., cards for articles or books, folders for chapters, whether notes are taken on a computer or not. The student should also know how to abstract an article to summarize the information contained. A reminder might be in order, though, that when in doubt whether to quote, the student should take down the material verbatim and decide later. The professor who makes sure the student knows how to search the literature efficiently helps the student focus on the research problem at hand and helps the student avoid bogging down in annoying and otherwise time-consuming clerical detail.

The literature review itself may be turned into a published state-of-the-art paper, making a valuable contribution to the literature. Students should be encouraged to publish their work as soon as possible when the problem investigated and the quality of the research will contribute to knowledge in the subject field.

Research Design and Methodology

The research design and methodology refers to the way the problem will be investigated. In the liberal arts, the design is often an outline or prospectus of the work. In the sciences, the methodology may be determined by the type of problem selected. The methodology may also be the focus of the research itself, i.e., the design of a new methodology to attack a particular problem. In the social sciences, the research design may be the most crucial part of the research project, actually driving data analysis and influencing research results. The professor should help the student determine what data will be meaningful, especially for the student's initial research project. The professor's goal is to help the student become an independent researcher. While this may mean letting the student make some mistakes and learn from them, the professor should try to maintain a balance between telling the student what to do and letting the student flounder and become discouraged.

Data Collection

Once the research design and methodology have been established and data collection begins, the professor's major role is to maintain the student's enthusiasm over a sometimes tedious aspect of the investigation. To maintain student enthusiasm the professor might meet and talk about some interesting aspects of the student's research and its implications. The professor should always give the student any new material that he comes across. Above all, the student needs support and encouragement when time schedules fall behind or other unexpected difficulties arise.

Some unexpected difficulties may require a revision in the research design, which may lead to more fruitful areas. Unexpected findings in the data may change the research into a pilot study leading to larger research projects to be undertaken at a later date.

Data Analysis

The research design may focus on the analysis of available data. Analysis of available data is often as important as analysis of new data collected for a project. Analysis takes data, newly collected or already available, and manipulates it to gain meaningful information. Students, especially in the social sciences, need to be reminded that negative findings from data analysis may be as important as positive findings.

Students usually need the professor's assistance as well as the assistance of statisticians and computer center personnel in data analysis. Students must learn how to present their findings in a form most easily understood and used by a prospective audience. Graphic data presentation is becoming an increasingly popular format for ease of understanding.

Writing

Urge the student to use a word-processor from the beginning of the research project to facilitate the inevitable revisions. Also remind the student to back up all work after each computer session. The time saved by this small effort can be immeasurable when Murphy's Law operates on the computer! In reviewing written work, take the role of the best peer reviewer and content editor, but don't dwell on editing for fine points of grammar and spelling.

Urge the student who has completed a quality research project to prepare a manuscript for publication in an appropriate journal. Guide the student through the manuscript submission and review process.

Professor-Student Authorship

No accepted guidelines exist for indicating the order of authors' names in collaborative authorship. The cynics say that the first author takes the credit and the second author has done the work! Basically, articles, books, and patents are intellectual property protected by copyright and patent law. Intellectual property is the stock-in-trade of the academic, contributing to prestige, status, promotion, tenure, consulting opportunities, etc. Therefore, the professor has a selfish interest in becoming the first author. The ethical dilemma arises from the professor's responsibility to promote student publication and to produce scholars. To what extent is a collaborative authorship the "property" of one person and to what extent is the authorship shared?

THESES AND DISSERTATIONS

Honors Papers and Theses

The requirements for these vary greatly from school to school and even between departments. There is an unfortunate tendency to have the honors paper or thesis be a long paper rather than a more substantive piece of research. Some colleges and universities, however, do try to have the student produce research resulting in a publishable paper for a refereed journal.

Dissertations

Written instructions about institutional policy governing rules for proposing, investigating, and defending a dissertation topic should be given to the student at the beginning of the doctoral program. In fairness to the student, once a proposal for investigating a topic has been accepted, his or her satisfactorily completed research should be recognized as fulfilling the dissertation requirement. Faculty questioning of the research topic and reservations about the research to be undertaken should be thoroughly aired and discussed during the time the proposal is being developed. The student's committee members are responsible for insuring that the student has completed a thorough review of all background and related research. The committee members are also responsible for insuring that the methodology developed for the research is the appropriate methodology for investigating this dissertation topic. These two parts of the dissertation process, the literature search for related research and the development of the methodology, should be satisfactorily completed before the student's dissertation proposal is formally accepted.

The chairman of the student's dissertation committee should assist the student in forming a dissertation committee by suggesting faculty interested in the student's proposed topic. These faculty members should also possess the expertise to insure that all aspects of the dissertation research, including the proposal, are monitored for thoroughness and accuracy. The committee members, ideally, should also be professors who work well together and have no political, ideological, or intellectual conflicts among themselves. Committee members should not grind any personal axes at the expense of the student.

In most institutions, the committee assists the student throughout the dissertation process, including preparation for defense of the completed research. The committee usually participates in examining the student's work at the defense. During any open-question session, committee members are well aware that their expertise is open to as much question as the student's own research efforts.

The mystique of the dissertation and the perceived magnitude of the project often overwhelm the student undertaking his or her first major research project. Some students are drained after preparing for and passing qualifying exams ("prelims") and need time to rest and recharge batteries. Other students have difficulty adjusting to the lack of formal course work. Still other students become bogged down by trying to complete dissertation research while working at a full-time job.

Getting the Student into Dissertation Gear

At many universities, an unfortunate gap develops between the end of formal course work and the selection of a dissertation advisor. The student, at this time, is left without support. Doctoral students should be encouraged to drop by and chat with a professor whose interests are congenial with theirs. Opportunities should be made available to doctoral students to build such relationships with several faculty members. These professors can then assist the student in the transition from course work to dissertation research. Some department chairmen review the progress of their doctoral students on a regular basis to see where they are in considering dissertation advisors and research topics. The doctoral students holding assistantships are fortunate in having continual and easy access to professors sharing mutual interests. For other students, the dissertation topic can sometimes be developed in a research methods course or as an outcome of preliminary investigations in a subject-related course. Some schools have dissertation seminars. Most schools recognize the need to prod or nudge a reluctant student to actually begin the dissertation process.

Advisor-Advisee Selection

The mutual selection of advisor and advisee is usually an informal process that depends on the student's area of research interest and on how well the two get along. The potential advisee may "shop" for advisors who may be interested in the student's proposed topic. The student may solicit a lot of informal advice from many faculty members.

University policy varies in reducing teaching loads for dissertation advising. The professor should be knowledgeable about policy in this area. While the professor has the obligation (as well the pleasure) to accept dissertation students, he also has the obligation to insure that the students being advised can expect a reasonable amount of time and attention during the dissertation process. This becomes especially difficult since the speed with which students will work is impossible to predict. The professor should keep track of all his dissertation students and prod excessively slow or inactive ones. Many times inactivity will result from a personal problem the student may be hesitant to discuss. At other times inactivity may result from some problem with the research itself. Problems in the latter area are usually more easily solved.

Selection of the Dissertation Topic

The doctoral student usually approaches the professor at the beginning of the dissertation process with a rather vague problem in the professor's area of interest. The first step is to build a working relationship with the student during the process of defining the dissertation problem (topic). The professor, after further discussion to refine and focus the problem, may express interest in assisting the student or refer the student to another professor who may have more expertise in the problem area the student would like to investigate. Students often select a problem that is too large to be manageable by one person. Such problems must be analyzed and a reasonable piece defined as a research topic. Some seemingly viable problems turn out to have been investigated by others. The responsible professor will use his subject-area expertise to direct the student into productive areas to avoid wasted time in discovering that a potential topic had already been investigated by others.

Once a professor accepts an advisee, the next step is to help the student form a dissertation committee. The committee is usually composed of three or four other members of the faculty plus one member from outside the department or the university. The expertise of each faculty and outside committee member should relate to the student's topic. The committee members' should possess complementary expertise. One member is often a statistician or an expert in the methodological aspects of the dissertation topic. The committee should work well together and set aside any personal disagreements that would hinder the student's progress.

The Proposal

Once the dissertation committee has been formed, the next task is to draft a proposal. The student's principal advisor acts as dissertation committee chairman and coordinates all aspects of the dissertation, including preparation and acceptance of the proposal. Each member of the committee is responsible for contributing his or her expertise as the proposal is developed. Once formally discussed and accepted at a meeting of the full committee, the proposal serves as a contract between the student and his or her dissertation committee. The proposal states the parameters and the background of the problem to be investigated, the need for the investigation, the methodology to be used in the investigation, and the hypotheses to be proved or disproved as a result of the investigation.

The Dissertation Prospectus

Some schools allow the student to develop a short (not more than five pages) statement about a proposed dissertation topic that can serve as a basis for discussion with the dissertation advisor, but which may be considered adequate as a proposal. Such a prospectus serves an equally useful purpose for discussing proposed research with funding agencies. The dissertation then proceeds as other research.

LEARNING BEYOND THE CLASSROOM

Work-Study

Many colleges and universities provide the opportunity for employment in conjunction with an academic program. Work-study differs from ordinary summer or semester work in that the college is active in providing the opportunity and that the work itself is supposed to be part of the student's learning experience. The work is a "real world" situation rather than a laboratory simulation.

However, the work-study experience often involves clerical routines rather than professional-level activity. The quality of the work-study experience depends, to a large extent, on both the initiative and interest of the student's supervisor and on the student's own initiative and attitude. All too often, though, learning goals are not articulated and the learning is not well integrated into the student's curriculum. Students do learn, though, that they do not want to remain very long at an entry or clerical level of employment. The work-study experience is often a more informal, one-time arrangement than the co-op experience, which is described below.

The Practicum

The practicum provides an opportunity in a real-life environment to apply the knowledge learned in class and/or the laboratory. The student is supervised on the job by a responsible individual who works in conjunction with the professor responsible for awarding academic credit for the practical experience.

Internship

Interning is a period of apprenticeship, sometimes legally required for licensure in a professional area. From the professor's point of view, the intern should learn, under close supervision, the range of activities in the field of study. One person should be in charge of supervising interns, though the intern may actually be apprenticed to a variety of instructors. The instructors each provide continual feedback to the internship supervisor on the intern's progress and performance.

Co-op Experience

A co-op (cooperative) experience generally involves a contractual relationship between an employer and a college or university for a specified work experience related to the student's major field of study. Colleges with formal co-op programs usually require the student to spend an extra (fifth) year to complete the undergraduate degree. An effective co-op program enables the student to earn money toward college expenses and to gain experience in his or her field of interest. Co-op programs can motivate the student to higher levels of effort or serve to change the student's mind about the occupational area in which he or she was interested. In either case, the student generally benefits from the experience. The college benefits from a constant interaction with potential employers for its graduates. This interaction enables the college to stay abreast of those attributes and skills considered most desirable in the current employment market.

•••••••••••••••

All students need to realize that learning, while often easy and fun, can also be difficult, hard work, and painful. The professor, as an independent study, research, thesis or dissertation advisor, can guide and manage and evaluate the individual student's learning. However, learning is a process in which the student must actively participate. Each student is, ultimately, personally responsible for the success or failure of the process.

Chapter **9**

MENTORING AND OTHER WAYS OF INTERACTING WITH STUDENTS

Mentoring, modeling, advising, monitoring, and other ways of interacting with students are not distinct categories. They merge and overlap. They can be formal or informal, planned or unplanned, conscious or unconscious. They are among the most important aspects of teaching. Despite the fact that formal advising has become an administrative responsibility in some colleges and universities, student-faculty interaction is today more and more emphasized as intrinsic to teaching excellence.

Mentoring, for purposes of this discussion, is broadly defined as the relationship between a professor and student. This relationship involves a two-way communication that may ignite in the student a desire to learn and grow, to be open and receptive to learning. The term "mentor" has an honored history as applied to the professor-student relationship. The term "mentoring" is more recent.

Mentoring has lately slipped in popular usage from defining a specific relationship to such generality that a textbook is sometimes said to be mentoring the reader through the topic. It is used here to refer to: (1) the relationship between a professor and the group of students in a class, and (2) the relationship between a professor and each individual student. Mentoring may grow through the college experience and often beyond. The mentoring relationship is valuable, unique, and rewarding for both professor and student. This relationship is more likely to develop when the professor is open and available to students both during a course and less formally outside of the classroom. Daloz characterizes the successful mentor as follows: "Mentors seem to do three fairly distinct types of things. They support, they challenge, and they provide vision" (p 212). This is a tall order which not every professor can achieve. However, awareness of the importance of mentoring to learning characterizes the true learning manager.

The role of mentor ranges from the distant in a large lecture class to the close when supervising a student in individual work. As in all relationships, the interactions involved in mentoring cannot be specified. The professor who does not undertake the role of mentor may as well disseminate her expertise through the impersonal medium of the textbook or television. The personal communication and relationship between professor and student is, for the student, one of the most valuable aspects of higher education.

One aspect of the professor's relationship with a student may be that of a *role model*. The student in a class may be having her first contact with, for instance, an anthropologist. What is an anthropologist like, and what does it mean to be an anthropologist? The average professor may not have thought of herself as representing the profession or field of knowledge. To what extent will the professor's values and behavior influence the student? These values may be especially important to the first or second year student who is still looking for a college major or a career choice.

The professor may also interact with a student as an *advisor*. The professor is a major contact in a world beyond the family, the high school, and frequently the student's home community. Advice may be sought about issues within a course, a curricular program, or a career choice. The student may wish to test thoughts and ideas about the world in general or about personal issues that require a more objective opinion than that available from friends or family.

Another part of the professor's job is to *monitor* student work. The professor's ability to interact with students by providing individual feedback about their work will vary with the size of the class. In large classes this feedback may be given by proxy through teaching assistants. However the feedback may be provided, the importance of early and frequent interaction with a professor or teaching assistant is essential to a student's progress and intellectual development.

Ideally, every student's learning process would be individualized to the student's particular needs and rate of progress. This is seldom possible because of the constraints of class size, time available to cover course material, and the time each student (and professor) has or chooses to devote to a particular course.

Out-of-class work provides the professor with more opportunity to monitor the progress of individual students. Courses with many small assignments scattered over the term enable the student to receive continual feedback. The professor is able to catch weak work early on, and indicate with detailed comments how work might be improved or suggest special tutoring in the course. The professor should encourage strong students with commentary elaborating on good points of the work and aspects of the subject that could be pursued further. In sum, mentoring includes alertness to student work in class and out, assistance to the student who comes for help, and attention to the student who needs help but hesitates to seek it.

ORIENTATION TO MENTORING
IN THE LEARNING PROCESS

Effective teachers, according to Guskey reporting research from six community colleges, are characterized by: (1) their use of planning, organization and cues; (2) positive regard for students; (3) encouragement of student participation; and (4) feedback, correctives, and reinforcement (pp 20-24). All of these characteristics are related to mentoring. Guskey reviews studies of student retention in college and concludes: "The provision of learning success ... is not only appropriate and alterable, it is also the most powerful motivational device available to a college professor" (p 79).

Learning success implies successful professor-student communication. The communication process, as modeled in information theory, includes feedback as a means of clarifying and substantiating information transfer between the sender and the receiver of a message. Not only should the professor provide feedback to students (both individually and as a group), but the professor should also be alert to feedback from students as part of the communication process.

John B. Carroll's model of learning states that the degree of learning is a function of the time spent divided by the time needed. The time spent is, in turn, a function of perseverance and the opportunity to learn. The time needed is a function of: (1) the learning rate, (2) the quality of instruction, and (3) the ability to understand the instruction. (Cited by Guskey pp 84-86). Many of these factors are influenced by the process of mentoring and interacting with students. Perseverance, particularly, is related to feelings of success and progress in learning; motivation is related to feelings that the student is being successful and is making progress.

121

Other factors that should be considered in preparing for mentoring include the diversity of the student body, the institutional environment, and various motivational factors. Each student must be considered a unique human being.

OPPORTUNITIES FOR MENTORING AND INTERACTING WITH STUDENTS

In the Classroom

Mentoring and interacting with students in the classroom can begin with noting who attends class irregularly or who is often late to class as simple clues to the need for early intervention to prevent potential learning problems. A student may decide, of course, that he or she can better spend class time in another way, but the professor should know that the student can still satisfactorily complete the course work. Attendance, however, can be overemphasized because it is so simple to determine. Some courses require more student participation than others. In those courses where student participation is not required (e.g., for the learning of other students), the professor needs to be assured that the student's time is better spent in other ways because of the student's learning style. Administrative requirements for attendance are a separate issue. When a large number of students stay away from the class, the professor should determine whether this is a reflection of her in-class teaching.

The attentiveness of students in class can be another way of determining the amount of interaction between professor and student. An attentive class is usually a class interested in absorbing the material being presented. Inattentiveness, on the other hand, may be caused by several factors, some of which may be beyond the professor's control. Boredom, for instance, may be caused by everything from the drone of a professor's monotonous voice to a student's overpreparedness in this aspect of the course. Information overload can be caused by the professor who presents too much material in one class period for a student to absorb. Work overload may be caused by the student who has undertaken more course work or outside activities than can be comfortably handled and is thinking of assignments not yet completed or other personal problems. General restlessness and shuffling may indicate that the class needs a break or is bored. Such general indications of inattentiveness provide feedback to the professor sensitive to these signals.

The professor interacting with students during a lecture may improve student attentiveness, learning, and listening skills by alerting the students, verbally and non-verbally, to various aspects of the lecture. Brown and Atkins suggest differentiating between openers, orientation to the lecture topic, key points (as opposed to extensions, examples, asides, and reservations) and the summaries (p 163).

The professor will want to check student preparedness for course work. The smaller the class, the more the professor can be aware of how prepared each student is both with sufficient background to comprehend course content and with sufficient work for each class session. Again, preparedness, or the lack of it, may be due as much to external factors as to a student's interest and abilities. Overzealous monitoring of preparedness may lead to frequent calling on unprepared students. A student should never be publicly embarrassed or ridiculed.

Student personality factors can be considered as the professor conducts a class. The hesitant student can be encouraged with nods and smiles. The overtalkative one can be redirected. In-class mentoring focuses on student reactions and preparation for the class, and emphasizes positive feedback.

On Assignments

Copious comments on all written work are very desirable. The professor should always be encouraging and prescriptive. The student should be complimented for doing well and shown how to do better. However, the ideal of detailed commentary must be balanced with the reality of the demands on the professor's time. This argues for multiple short assignments that are distributed across the semester or which may form parts of a megaproject due at the end. Multiple small assignments give the student an opportunity to learn from mistakes and to improve during the course. They also ease the burden on the instructor. Obviously, assignments should always be returned as quickly as possible.

Instructions for assignments ought to be clear and specific. Instructions should not only be written, but an opportunity should also be provided in class for clarification. Too many questions about assignments, however, may indicate reluctance, stalling, or anxiety. A time must come to stop talking about the assignment and begin doing it.

Writing assignments can be particularly difficult. Good writing is a craft that is, usually, not inborn. To write well, students must understand the assignment and, possibly, read or research the topic so it is well in mind. Before starting to write, the student needs to consider the potential audience for the written work. At this point the student can begin to plan and organize the writing and work on a draft. Once written, the draft should be reviewed, evaluated, and revised. Opportunities for interacting with the student's work can occur at each step, sometimes through an intermediate writing assignment that can be incorporated into the final work. The learning manager will want to consider how much time to spend orienting the class to written assignments. Sometimes an explanatory handout is helpful. Suggestions for dividing written assignments into component parts are given in the assignments chapter.

With Reading

Some students, especially first year students, do not know how to read for college classes. These students are different from those who enter college ill-prepared with inadequate reading skills. The ill-prepared student may need to be referred for remediation to the college facility responsible for helping with study skills.

Brown and Atkins differentiate six levels of reading: (1) scanning for specific information, (2) skimming for a quick impression, (3) surveying to determine what is covered, (4) light study reading which is essentially passive, (5) directed reading which is actively reading for specific purposes, and (6) deep study reading to "make connections, meaning, consider implications, and to evaluate argument" (p 173). Many students have never been required to do more than light reading. Orienting students to different levels of reading is helpful. Assignments may also be specifically directed so that students have the purpose of the reading clearly in mind. The SQ3R method provides another helpful approach to reading. SQ3R stands for Survey, Question, Read, Recite and Review. SQ3R is especially helpful for attacking intensive reading assignments in textbooks when a lot of information needs to be internalized.

By Helping with Problem Solving

Mentoring can involve helping students to solve problems. Cognitive science is showing that there are standard strategies for problem-solving. These strategies may be goal-directed, heuristic, and algorithmic. Brown and Atkins list four stages in problem solving that may be helpful for students. The first stage involves clarification of the problem. This includes dissecting the problem statement, representing the problem graphically or figuratively, looking for subproblems, and stating the problem clearly. In the second stage, the student determines how the problem is to be approached. This includes thinking about possible procedures, looking for analogies, and considering different alternatives. The third stage is solving the problem. This may entail a variety of problem solving methods. In the fourth stage, the results are checked and evaluated (pp 184-191).

During Office Hours

Most professors schedule certain office hours during the week and are also available by appointment. Conferences may be scheduled during the term. In some courses, especially seminars, the professor may schedule conferences in place of one or more class sessions. Office hours provide a range of opportunities for individual faculty-student interaction. Sometimes the student wants to discuss an idea with the professor. At other times a student may wish advice about curriculum planning or job opportunities. The discussion may also be tutorial in terms of a particular course. The professor, however, has limited time for tutoring and may, instead, refer the student to the campus facility for study skills.

Other Course-related Opportunities for Mentoring

Laboratory work provides many opportunities for interacting with students. Individual research can involve a close mentoring relationship. Brief conferences just before or after class are often useful. Many students will stop to clarify small points at these times.

MENTORING ASSISTANTS

Teaching assistants may be available to help students in large classes. Teaching assistants may have appointments as instructors or lecturers. They are frequently graduate students. In some places, undergraduates have been used successfully as teaching assistants. Mentoring with teaching assistants is twofold: the professor's indirect mentoring of the class and individual students via the teaching assistants and the direct mentoring of students by the teaching assistants themselves. Often teaching assistants serve as leaders of discussion sections or discussion groups.

Teaching assistants need to be clear about their role. They also need to be trained and guided. They should attend the professor's lectures and meet regularly with the professor to discuss any problems that have arisen and to give the professor feedback from the students. Segerstrale discusses the multifaceted role of the section leader from the point of view of the teaching assistant. She discusses how to cope with conflicting loyalties as well as how to make sections useful (Segerstrale).

Janssen describes the use of undergraduate teaching assistants (TAs) at Cornell University in a large (1,200 students) psychology class. TAs are recruited by interview from those who have completed the course, done well and have a high grade point average. The TAs meet for an organizing session, before summer vacation and again just before the class starts in the fall, to be sure they are prepared to lead discussion groups that are part of the class. The TAs are video-taped for feedback on their teaching assistance in the beginning of the term and often later in the semester. Both graduate and under-graduate TAs gather frequently in the psychology department lounge to gossip and informally exchange ideas with the professor in charge of the class (Janssen).

Laboratory assistants, and, sometimes, research assistants serve a similar role in mentoring students while they in turn are being men-tored. The relationship between teaching assistants, laboratory assis-tants and research assistants frequently becomes very close. They and the professor may form a highly cohesive group.

INTERACTING WITH ATYPICAL STUDENTS

The learning of the brilliant student, the plodder, the foreign stu-dent, and the physically handicapped student may require special attention. The professor who can channel disruptive behavior into more productive efforts will often find that the over-talkative student, the confrontational student, the whisperer, and the class clown may become positive assets to the class. These students are also likely to take other courses that a professor offers and continue to contribute positively to the classroom experience. Discipline problems, per se, seldom arise in higher education.

The Brilliant Student

The brilliant student presents both opportunity and danger to the professor in a classroom situation. The professor has the opportunity to motivate and guide the brilliant student beyond the scope of the course in his or her learning and research. In addition, the skillful professor will be able to draw on the knowledge and efforts of the brilliant student to enrich the class as a whole and to add an extra dimension to the course. The danger lies in teaching to the level of the brilliant student and losing the rest of the class; or, conversely, in teaching to the level of the class and boring or turning off the brilliant student by failing to challenge his or her intellect.

The brilliant student does indeed require an extra effort in personal instruction and guidance from the professor. However, the effort and the opportunity to challenge and guide a brilliant mind provides most professors with a high degree of personal satisfaction.

A few professors, sadly, will resent the intellectual abilities of the brilliant student and see this student as a negative challenge to their own knowledge and authority. This reaction to a brilliant student is unsatisfactory from any point of view. Any professor with expertise in a subject area should certainly be able to guide the brilliant student to sources of information beyond the ability of the class as a whole to absorb. That professor would also enable the class to benefit from the brilliant student's knowledge and experience and to enrich the course for everyone involved.

The Plodding Student

The plodder achieves by perseverance what other students achieve more easily. However, the self-discipline exhibited by the plodder is needed for career success after graduation. The caring professor never disregards the plodder, although, like the brilliant student, the plodder will require individual attention beyond that given to the class as a whole.

The plodder may require more detailed explanations and, at times, a more simplified explanation than the class as a whole. In assisting the plodder, the conscientious professor often discovers an improvement in her own communication skills which will benefit other students and future classes.

Some plodders will test a professor's patience by asking innumerable questions in class. The professor should be cautioned that the plodder is probably not the only person in the class who has the very same question, but is the one person whose persistence and determination to be successful requires that his or her questions be answered. Where a class can be enriched by the additional knowledge of the brilliant student, a class that has a plodder can be enriched by constant reinforcement and clarification of its learning.

The Over-talkative Student

The over-talkative student usually behaves in one or more of the following ways:

• By frequent or continual sotto voice or whispered commentary to nearby students while the professor or other students are trying to talk;

• By dominating a question period;

• By interrupting or adding a personal comment to every discussion;

• By attempting to engage the professor in a dialogue that is not relevant to the interests of other students or to the objectives of the class.

This behavior is generally annoying to other students and distracting, at best, to the learning process for the class. Depending on the personality of the over-talkative student, the professor must find ways to restrain and to channel the disruptive aspects of the student's over-talkative ways.

The Confrontational Student

Some students feel the need to adopt a confrontational attitude toward their professor. This attitude may be the result of a personality conflict between student and professor or may result from a student's personality problem. In any case, the confrontational student poses a difficult problem with no simple solution. The professor might be wise to seek advice from other faculty about their experiences with the student and suggestions about effective techniques for minimizing the problem. In extreme cases, intervention by the college or university's counseling services might be required. The professor should realize that the confrontational student might also be a litigious student. The professor must try to minimize the confrontation while seeking to resolve the difficulties causing it..

Whispering

Whispering has several causes ranging from student boredom and inattention to an inability to hear or understand the professor. The over-talkative student can also be a habitual whisperer. In any case, the professor should determine the cause of the whispering and then take some appropriate action. The class should not be penalized by the disruptive, distracting whispering caused by a bored, inattentive, or over-talkative student.

The Class Clown

Some students seek the center of attention by clowning at every opportunity during class. The occasional clown is harmless and can offer a momentary distraction that is both amusing and relaxing for the whole class. Carried to extremes, however, clowning can distract from the learning process and should be treated in the same manner as whispering.

The Foreign Student

A foreign student is usually considered a student from a country other than the one in which he or she is studying. In the United States, a student from another English-speaking country might be considered a "foreign student" because the customs and, to some extent, the vocabulary differ from one English-speaking country to another. The British use of a simple word such as "lift," meaning elevator, can be confusing to the American. A foreign student must adapt to customs in an American college or university that may be very different from the customs in his or her home country. Adapting to contemporary spoken and written American English may be the easiest of the adjustments which a foreign student will make.

The casual and familiar camaraderie between students and faculty at an American college or university can be difficult for a student to understand and get accustomed to. The right to question the professor or to challenge a point made by the professor would never be allowed in the higher education systems of many countries. The skills required for critical thinking and analysis are new to many foreign students who have been taught only to memorize and to regurgitate without question the material provided by the "expert" professor.

A foreign student from a non-English speaking country often has more difficulty with spelling and grammar than a student whose dominant language is English. The student should expect to see corrections made in spelling and grammar, but the foreign student's ability to master the course content should be the professor's main focus in evaluation. The professor should be aware of and sensitive to the many adjustments which the foreign student must make for one very important reason. The professor must realize that she will form part of the total impression of the host country and its citizens that the foreign student will take back to his or her native land. Many foreign students return home to become powerful citizens in their own land. Their impressions from their educational experience abroad undoubtedly influence their attitude about and their decisions concerning the country or countries where they studied.

The Physically Handicapped Student

The physically handicapped student is generally one of the most conscientious and hard-working students, determined to graduate despite a handicap. Most students who are physically handicapped learn to make each faculty member aware of their abilities and physical limitations. These limitations may require some flexibility from the professor. For instance, a blind student may need to be given tests orally. A student with hearing difficulties may wish to record each class and amplify lecture and discussions at home.

Absenteeism is rarely a problem since most physically handicapped students have developed back-up systems to enable them to keep abreast of class work and course requirements.

Attendance and Absenteeism

Taking attendance every class period in a college or university setting seems a waste of time after the first week, when it is necessary to establish the class roster and to learn students' names. Each professor, though, should decide how important regular attendance is to her course and establish some attendance policy.

Absenteeism caused by student illness becomes a matter for individual consultation and adjustment depending on the length of the absence, its cause, and the amount of work to be made up. Monitoring attendance may alert the professor to potential problems.

Make-up Classes, Tests and Exams

Unless the professor establishes a policy at the beginning of the course for make-up classes, tests and exams, some students may abuse the professor's good nature and lack of policy. Make-up classes requiring extra effort should be strictly limited to emergency situations. Some students will ask for make-up tests and exams to avoid studying for the scheduled test/exam by asking those students who did take the test/exam about the questions on it. The best way to avoid this problem is to establish a policy of no make-up tests and exams. Such a policy enables the professor to give a make-up test/exam in a real emergency situation where student's prior efforts merit some professorial compassion and compromise. Such a policy also enables the professor to adopt a tougher stance with the lazy or disinterested student.

Plagiarism and Cheating

(See Chapter 13.)

Miscellaneous Problems

Miscellaneous problems, which can affect the behavior of the whole class, can usually be circumvented by general departmental policy or by individual policy stated in the professor's syllabus for the course. These problems include those caused by alcohol and substance abuse, absenteeism, and by the request for make-up classes and make-up tests. Frequently, the professor may need to refer students with such problems to student health, academic advising, or another student support service. The professor may wish to make the appropriate support service aware of potential problems in these areas. When necessary, the professor always has the right to dismiss a student from a class session.

INFORMAL OPPORTUNITIES FOR INTERACTING WITH STUDENTS

As a mentor, the professor will want to take advantage of the many informal opportunities outside of the classroom for interacting with students. Club meetings, social events, and many other non-academic activities offer ways for professors and students to become acquainted on a more informal basis than is possible in the classroom or office.

The fact that relationships develop in a positive way while sharing food or drink is common knowledge. While eating in the classroom may be a distraction to the professor and to other students, sharing food and drink with students outside of the classroom is one of the easiest and most effective ways to enable students to know faculty members as "people." Conversely, it is one of the most pleasurable ways for the professor to get to know students.

The professor who has developed an informal relationship with students has usually at the same time developed a special trust and rapport that goes beyond learning management in the classroom. Such a relationship often continues beyond graduation with the professor serving as a mentor, friend, and perhaps colleague. Interacting with students as a mentor, the professor provides praise and encouragement as well as constructive criticism in evaluating student performance apart from her more formal evaluative role, which is discussed in the following chapter.

Chapter **10**

EVALUATION

The evaluation essential to assessing the effectiveness of learning management has several aspects. These include evaluation of the course and its materials, evaluation of the student and the class, and evaluation of the professor. The course and its materials are evaluated in terms of their value in a particular curriculum. The student is evaluated in terms of his or her progress in learning course content and in comparison to the learning of others in the class. The professor is evaluated in terms of the value or excellence of his teaching as well as in terms of student response to the course.

In his continual evaluation of the course and its materials, the professor should be asking the following questions:

• How well is the course meeting the needs of the students currently enrolled?

• How does this course relate to other courses and to changes in other courses?

• How effective are the materials (textbooks, audiovisuals, and courseware) in helping the student achieve the course goals and objectives?

• What newly produced materials have been evaluated and/or previewed for incorporation into the course design?

• How much do the class activities contribute to student learning?

• Could any of these activities be improved or should some different activities be considered?

The professor, as well as the college or university administration, will want the students to evaluate the course. The assumption is made that although students take the course to learn subject content, they will know at the end of the course just how much they have learned from the course and its materials, how well the professor can communicate subject content, and how well the professor motivated them to learn. This assumption depends upon the course. Sometimes students can-

133

not see the actual impact of the course until much later. The professor's ability to motivate learning is especially vital in required courses which the students might not otherwise take.

The course will also be evaluated for subject content by the department during periodic curricular revisions to update a departmental program and to monitor the sequencing of course content from lower level to higher level courses. In addition to student and departmental course evaluations, accrediting visitations also examine and evaluate course syllabi and often offer positive constructive feedback.

After each class, the professor may wish to assess student response to and understanding of the class objectives:

• Which objectives seemed to be of most interest?

• Which objectives seemed to be most clearly understood?

• Which objectives may need to be reinforced or clarified at the beginning of the next class?

• How is the class as a whole responding to the course, to the professor's personality, and to his way of presenting course materials?

Evaluation of the professor is discussed in Chapter 13. This includes student evaluations of the professor's teaching, the professor's self-evaluation, and the evaluative process involved in professorial reappointment, promotion, and tenure.

Evaluation can and should be used to enhance the performance of every student. Students want to know how well they are doing and what they need to do to improve their performance. The professor monitors the learning process and gives frequent feedback about what still needs to be learned and how to learn it. Learning theory shows that students need to have clear goals (i.e., to know what is to be learned and the steps to learn it). Students need to experience success— successful experiences build the self-concept basic to motivation. This motivation leads to persevering in learning tasks. Students need feedback about how to adjust and improve their performance. Effective learning management uses frequent immediate, specific, and prescriptive evaluation (Guskey, pp 31-45). Prescriptive evaluation guides the students "in terms of how they can remedy their learning errors, and how they can overcome the learning difficulties they may be experiencing" (Guskey p 35). This chapter is divided into three main topics: first, the evaluative process; second, commonly evaluated aspects of student performance; and third, compassionate counterpoints.

THE EVALUATIVE PROCESS

Student progress in learning the subject area should be monitored and evaluated throughout the course. A thorough evaluation of student learning includes an objective assessment of the student's performance in class and on assignments, tests, papers, and projects. The evaluation may also be influenced by the professor's more subjective knowledge of the student's efforts as a result of personal interaction during the class period, office hours, etc. At the end of the course, the professor must give the student a grade and, perhaps, write a comment for the student's file or a letter of recommendation.

DATA AND ITS APPLICATION TO STUDENT FEEDBACK

The more contacts the professor has with the student, the more data can be generated for evaluation. Data are inputs to the evaluative process. As any input, data can be misleading and must be interpreted with care. During the evaluative process, the data being gathered can be used diagnostically to monitor student progress as well as to determine and to remedy student problems with learning subject content. Opportunities for direct professor-student contact vary with the class level and the class size. Specific data-generating opportunities for evaluation occur in class work, out-of-class assignments, laboratories, testing, and papers and projects. Students tend to consider evaluation solely as graded work. The professor might better regard evaluation as many opportunities to encourage and provide feedback to students so that the students can and will do their best work in an atmosphere of clear learning goals. Ideally, students should expect and believe that the grades which result from the professor's evaluative process are earned symbols of learning, of achievement during the course, or of a skill level attained as a result of the course.

LEARNING IN RELATION
TO COURSE GOALS AND OBJECTIVES

Evaluation should generally be based on student learning in terms of the goals and objectives of the course. The goals and objectives should include both the formal goals and objectives stated in the syllabus and the professor's personal goals and objectives for the course and for the students. One obvious focus is the behavioral objectives or performance asked of the students, i.e., the actual change in student learning or behavior as a result of the course. Evaluation is the converse of planning. Planning determines what learning the student should accomplish during the course. Evaluation determines what levels of learning the student actually attained. When a goal of the course is improvement in a specified subject, the professor must determine the level of student knowledge when the course began. This determination can usually be accomplished by a pre-test. Sometimes the course goal refers only to knowledge exhibited at the end of the course. In this case, the student may have known the material before starting and, perhaps, should have exempted the course.

Educational evaluators differentiate between the engineering and medical evaluation models. In the engineering model, input and output characteristics are assessed. In the medical or systems analysis approach, "the interrelatedness of all the factors (psychological, social, environmental, and education) which may affect performance" are dealt with (Anderson, et al.). Side effects include the difference between intended and possible outcomes. The medical mode also focuses on the processes that produce the observed changes (pp 245-246). In learning management, the medical evaluation model is a useful analogy. Things occur that may not be specified in the goals and objectives. They need to be assessed. The concept of diagnosis is extremely helpful in the monitoring of individual students as well as in monitoring all other objects of evaluation.

DISTINGUISHING BETWEEN
EVALUATION AND MEASUREMENT

Measurement and evaluation are not synonymous. Evaluation is a much broader concept than measurement. Measurement implies an objectivity and a standard. *The Encyclopaedia of Educational Evaluation* points out that measurement yields data which may be helpful in evaluation, but which are not themselves the same as evaluation (Anderson et al., p 137). Measurement requires well-established standards and criteria for comparison (pp 98-104).

Validity and reliability should be considered in all evaluation. Validity implies that the evaluative criterion is a true reflection of the learning to be evaluated. For example, time taken to finish writing an in-class essay would not be a valid criterion to evaluate the student's writing ability. The evaluative criteria should be appropriate to the goals and objectives of the course and not selected because they are easy to use. The professor could take a student's IQ or previous experience with a subject and probably come up with some correlation with course performance; however, this correlation would not reflect the learning accomplished during the course. Similarly, class participation may be more indicative of a student's style (talkativeness) than of learning, or even of interest. In establishing evaluative criteria, the professor needs to distinguish between measurement and evaluation and to establish relevant, objective criteria for evaluation.

Reliability refers to consistency. If the same evaluative measure were to be repeatedly applied, would the results be the same? Reliability and validity (simply touched upon here) are treated in more depth in any social science statistics or research methods text.

TESTING

While evaluation is applied to many aspects of student work in and out of class (including assignments, laboratory work, papers and projects, independent studies, internships and co-op programs), formal tests are associated with measurable data that can be gathered by various techniques and types of questions. These tests are designed in different ways depending on their purpose but should not be limited to testing the student's ability to memorize factual information. Such testing was developed to be completely objective and easy to score both manually and by machine. In practice, testing is often limited to the simplest forms of cognitive knowledge, i.e., the ability to recognize or recall specific facts and terminology. This ability is important. However, the goals and objectives of a course might also include more complex cognition, in addition to recognition and recall. This cognition could include comprehension, application, analysis, synthesis, and evaluation of course content. (Note: See Appendix B.) In any case the outcome of testing or evaluation usually results in a series of grades during the course and in a final grade for the course itself.

A major issue in developing tests is the difficulty in establishing test validity and reliability. The professor tries to develop tests that reflect and assess goals and objectives (i.e., tests that are valid), questions that are not misleading, that discriminate among levels of student achievement, and that "work" in different sections of the course. While a test may be a reliable measure of achievement, the professor must be aware of the limitations of tests.

TYPES OF QUESTIONS:—
Testing for Recognition and Recall

Facts and information to which a student has been exposed are easier to recognize when they are presented with some clue. Recognition questions provide suggestions about answers. Recall questions require the student to remember facts and information without having them suggested by the question itself. For example, in a question where the student must match the facts in Column A with the information in Column B, all the information which a student must have is presented in the question itself. On the other hand, a question that asks a student to list a chronology of historical events would depend completely on the student's ability to recall this chronology from memory without other clues from the question itself. Scoring or grading both types of questions is usually based on the number of correct answers. Scoring of recognition questions may be more reliable but less valid than scoring of recall questions. However, recognition questions can be more easily scored by machine. Both recognition and recall questions are frequently used on quizzes and tests.

☐ Recognition:

The three most common ways of testing for recognition are true-false, matching, and multiple-choice questions. Recognition questions are useful for emphasizing and reinforcing information and may also be used for testing comprehension and application.

True-false questions are constructed with a phrase or sentence that requires a true or false answer. These questions appear easy to construct, but students frequently misinterpret them. A good true-false set of questions is extremely difficult to construct. Students like them because they can be answered quickly. Professors like them because they are easy to correct.

Matching questions are constructed with a list of answers and a list of questions to which the answers are to be matched. The two lists should be short enough (about ten answers) so that students can keep them both in mind. At times, more answers can be listed than questions. Matching questions, like true-false questions, can be answered quickly and are easy to correct.

Multiple-choice questions are constructed by providing a choice of responses to a phrase. One of the responses should complete the phrase most accurately or precisely, giving the correct answer to the question. Multiple-choice questions are subject to misinterpretation, especially when the choice of response depends on a degree of precision. However, they can usually be answered quickly and are easy to correct.

☐ Recall:

The most common ways of testing for recall are fill-in-the-blank questions and short-answer questions. Recall questions, like recognition questions, can be used to emphasize and reinforce information as well as to test comprehension and application of learning.

Fill-in-the-blank questions are constructed using a sentence with one or more blanks, usually indicated by an underline, which may or may not indicate the length of the appropriate response. The student must recall the most appropriate word or phrase to fill the blank(s) so the sentence makes a correct statement. These questions can usually be answered quickly, although they are subject to misinterpretation. They are easy to correct.

Short-answer questions are constructed by phrasing the questions so that they may be answered by one or more words, a short phrase, a definition, or a one or two sentence description or explanation. Questions may be constructed to ask the student to "identify" artifacts or specimens in science courses, paintings and sculpture in art history courses, musical compositions, etc. Questions may ask the student for a brief definition of a concept or for a brief explanation of a particular phenomenon. These questions can often be answered quickly and are usually easy to correct. They are less subject to misinterpretation than other types of recognition and recall questions.

Testing for Critical Thinking and Problem-Solving

Questions can also be asked on tests and examinations to assess student ability to think critically and to solve problems. Such questions require that the student apply learning in new ways and to new and different material. Questions may be constructed which require not only problem-solving but also a description of the method used to reach the solution. Questions may be constructed requiring the student to synthesize a body of data or to evaluate evidence. Answers to such questions may be brief or lengthy. Credit may be given for the correct approach to an answer to critical thinking and problem-solving questions as well as for the correct answer to the question.

Objective questions may be designed as variations on the types described for recognition and recall of learning. For instance, true-false questions may require the student to provide the correct answer to those questions where the response is "false." The student can also be asked to explain why he or she has responded to a question as "true" or "false."

All the types of tests mentioned above can also be used to test critical thinking. However, to test productive thinking, the questions are generally longer and more difficult. Questions involving interpretation of maps or graphs may be asked. Questions may also require analysis of a paragraph. They may call for solving a multi-step problem. Often the data to be used are given in the question, and the student must employ the methods, theories, and problem-solving approaches he or she has learned to answer correctly.

Such objective tests are time-consuming and difficult to construct. The professor may wish to take advantage of items available in various texts or use problems posed in recent journal articles. Items developed for review by testing services, such as the Graduate Record Examination, are usually reliable. Like all objective examinations, the questions can be graded quickly. True-false and multiple-choice questions can be scored by machine.

Essay questions are frequently constructed to assess the extent and depth of a student's learning as well as to assess the student's ability to write grammatically correct standard English. Questions may be general or specific, depending on the amount of material to be tested, the professor's objectives, and the number of questions to be answered in an allotted time. The questions should be clearly stated and directly related to the purposes of the course. They may pose new situations that draw, for answers, upon materials learned. The questions should not ask about obscure information or about material that was not emphasized in class. The professor's instructions for an essay test should include the criteria that will be used to evaluate the answers. The answers to the questions may be brief or lengthy depending on the professor's instructions, the number of questions, and the time allotted.

Essay questions can cover a range of topics. They force students to organize information and to be concise and precise in their answers. Essay questions can be constructed to allow students to use their text and notebooks to answer. Such questions require that the student think critically and synthesize a body of information. They also encourage original thinking, since every student may be required to take and justify a unique personal perspective with specific information. Questions requiring lengthy answers enable the student to demonstrate overall grasp of the subject and the ability to write well. Answers to essay questions are always time-consuming to correct; however, written comments about the student's answers—praising well-written answers and correcting errors and omissions—can guide the student in learning. See also the criteria for evaluating papers in the section Evaluating Papers and Projects.

PURPOSES OF DIFFERENT TYPES OF TESTS:—

Test questions can be constructed by the professor or taken from various texts. The professor should be aware that students have a fast and accurate communication network. Each section of each class will be well aware of questions the professor has asked on quizzes, tests, and examinations for the past several terms. Many fraternities and sororities keep files of quizzes, tests, and examinations which their members have taken. Fraternity and sorority members using these files to study often have a testing edge over students who are not fraternity and sorority members.

Students study more effectively for a test, and generally score better, when they know the type of questions which will be asked: multiple-choice, essay, true-false, etc. Quiz, test, and examination questions should relate to the stated course objectives. Students should not be tested on obscure bits of information unless memorization of trivia is one of the course objectives. As Erickson points out, "The only instructional sin greater than teaching obsolete or trivial information is to test and grade students about such knowledge." (Erickson, pp 13-14).

Quiz

The quiz is an informal test which usually has a minimal impact on a student's grade. It is frequently used to reinforce student learning and to measure student progress in learning the course content. A quiz usually takes no more than half a class period. It may be written and given to the entire class. It may also be oral, with each student answering one or more questions, followed by class discussion of the answer.

A quiz can be given at the beginning or end of the class period. Since students always finish any kind of test at different times, the professor may wish to set a specific time when all quizzes will be collected, finished or not. Because students usually finish a quiz at different times, timing the class activities may be difficult when a quiz is given at the beginning of the period. When a quiz is given at the beginning of the period, the professor can immediately discuss the correct answers and then continue with the topic of the day. A previously announced quiz given at the end of the period may distract student concentration during the day's class activity. Students may be too nervous about the quiz to focus on the class material. They may also try to study for the quiz during class.

Quizzes are especially useful for giving early feedback during a unit of study. A quiz may be given as early as the second week of classes. The announcement of a forthcoming quiz can give the professor the opportunity to indicate the kind and level of work expected in the course. The weak student is given early warning; the stronger student is given early reassurance.

Quizzes are especially useful for cumulative material where the next step in the material cannot be understood without a thorough grounding in earlier material. Mathematics, science, and foreign languages are common subjects where quizzes are useful to students and professor alike. Quizzes are also useful for assessing knowledge of specific facts and of ways and means of dealing with specific facts. Some professors will spring quizzes, unannounced, on their classes; however, students should be warned from the first day of the course that such unannounced quizzes will occur.

Some professors state in their syllabi that a certain percentage of the final grade will be derived from quizzes. In courses where quizzes are frequent, the professor may choose to omit the lowest quiz grade from the calculation of the quiz component of the student's final grade.

Test

The test is a more formal means of measuring student performance. It is more heavily weighted in determining a student's final course grade than a quiz, but less heavily weighted than an examination. A test usually takes a full class period. Many professors formally or informally review with the class the material which the test will cover. End-of-unit tests are sometimes substituted for mid-term examinations. A test generally consists of written responses to the questions.

Examination

An examination is more formal and heavily weighted than a test in determining the student's final grade for a course. Colleges and universities usually give an examination to the class at the middle and at the end of the term. These examinations may be designed to determine a student's ability to retain facts, to analyze problems, or to synthesize information presented in class with information independently gathered by the student outside of class. Examinations are rarely used to measure creativity, although originality of response may be a scoring criterion. Examinations, especially the final examination, are often considered a major component of the evaluation process.

Examinations generally require written responses to the professor's questions. Oral examinations are rarely used at the undergraduate or master's levels. They are customary for defense of doctoral dissertations and frequently used for defense of doctoral research proposals. On the rare occasions when oral examinations are given at the undergraduate level, they may be substituted for a written examination for a handicapped student or for a student with a broken arm, etc. Some handicapped students may arrange to turn in a taped transcript of their answers.

Take-home Test

The take-home test is especially useful for open-book testing and when use of the library becomes necessary to answer the questions. A take-home test allows more time for classroom instruction. Professors giving take-home tests may require the student to turn in typewritten answers. Students answering take-home questions should be expected to cooperate with each other and to discuss their responses. This may be a useful aspect of learning course content, but makes the interpretation of answers more difficult. Take-home tests enable students to answer the questions in a more relaxed atmosphere and without the time constraints of the classroom. However, the amount of time permitted for a take-home test should be short.

Pre- and Post-Tests

Pre- and post-tests to evaluate student performance have not seen wide use in colleges and universities. These tests are useful in skill-related courses such as language courses, computer programming courses, etc. In courses like these, a student's knowledge level can be tested with a pre-test for placement in a beginning, intermediate, or advanced level course. Upon completing the course, the student's learning is measured by a post-test to determine whether or not the student has learned the skills which the course was intended to develop.

Another use of the pre-test at the college and university level is to give the student an idea of some of the information he or she will learn from the course. This pre-test may be a part of the syllabus, but not taken in class. The post-test, then, would reinforce the student's learning of the answers to the pre-test questions.

PREPARING STUDENTS TO TAKE TESTS AND EXAMINATIONS:—

Preparation for tests gives students an opportunity to review, with the professor, material covered in the course. Tests may be used to assist comprehension and application of concepts to new material. Students may sometimes prepare more effectively for a test when they are given a set of possible questions ahead of time which define the scope of the test and the type of questions to be asked.

Preparation for examinations allows the students to step back and look at what they have covered by mid-term or at the end of a term. This preparation should involve analysis and synthesis of course material. Examinations are almost always more general and comprehensive than tests. Examinations should be a useful and helpful culmination of the learning experience. However, student fear of examinations, generated by their weight in the grading process, too often overcomes any additional value they may have as a component of the learning experience.

The professor sensitive to student fears about examinations tries to ameliorate these anxieties with cautions about putting off studying for the exam or overstudying. Many students actually believe that they have not learned as much as they should or have not studied as much as they should. They are certain that, in taking the examination, these perceived inadequacies will become as clear to the professor as they are to the student. The sensitive professor knows that some students are indeed poor test takers and, for these students, evaluation of in-class work and assignments should weigh heavily in the grading process. The sensitive professor also reminds students that the exam, although a major part of the course grade, is still only one part of term's work and of the learning experience.

GRADING

In grading, the professor needs to consider three different responsibilities: the responsibility to the student, the responsibility to the college or university, and the responsibility to the world at large. The student needs to know how well he or she is doing in relationship to other students and to the goals and objectives for the particular course. The institution has certain standards and reputation; a grade from a school means something. The world at large includes employers and others; they assume a certain knowledge base as the result of taking a course. The employer expects a student to be prepared to undertake certain tasks as the result of taking a course. All three of these responsibilities must be considered. It .does the student no favor to allow the belief that he or she has a level of preparation that is not up to expected standards.

Grading is so significant to the student as an evaluative measure of performance that grades should not be awarded lightly. Students should know, from the first session of the course, how their learning will be evaluated, what criteria the professor will use to determine grades for specific assignments, and the weight to be given to various aspects of their work in determining the final grade for the course. The professor should communicate this information to the class in the written syllabus.

Grades usually represent the student's relative performance in relation to some standard. Grades can also represent a level of mastery.

Scores, particularly on tests, are not the same as grades. The professor must decide how to translate a score into a grade. Grades may be awarded on the basis of a standard. In this case, it is possible for all students to achieve an A. Another common approach compares students to each other, awarding a certain percentage of each grade level to students scoring within a certain range. Using this approach, even students scoring 40-50% can receive an A. Comparative grading is frequently used for papers and projects. Often scoring is not the issue for papers and projects; grades are awarded by comparing student achievements based on various stated criteria. Blind scoring of tests, i.e., hiding the students' identity from the reader of the test, may be used for more objective grading. Grades may also be awarded on the basis of contracts; in such cases, students receive a certain grade by satisfactorily completing a specified amount of work. Extra-credit can be a variation on contracting.

Grading "on the curve" refers to the bell-shaped curve of the statistical normal distribution. Usually, however, grading "on the curve" does not refer to giving as many A's as F's, but to the grades given at the upper end of the distribution. Thus a C is passing. B is above average and A is excellent; D's and F's are exceptions. If the professor were to strictly follow the normal distribution, about 69% of the class grades would be in the C range, about 13% each for the B and D range, and about 2 1/2% each for A's and F's. There may be institutional or departmental norms for the percent of each grade level. In practice, the percent of A's and B's may be higher even than the percentages suggested by using only the upper end of the distribution.

Other distributions and numerical manipulations are also used. The professor must consider what these scores mean. When one-half point makes a difference in a grade level, the grade is questionable. The professor should consider the contribution of scores to evaluation in general. What relationship do the scores have to the achievement of the goals and objectives of the course?

Despite common knowledge that some students are poor test takers, in-class work (including tests) is helpful in determining the validity of independent out-of-class work. Poor performances, especially early in the term, may be discarded in determining the final grade. Indeed, an improved performance may be indicative of learning. Little purpose is served by averaging in a zero or 20% score with an overall excellent performance. By the same token, learning or improvement is not synonymous with high achievement.

Some professors determine grades only by objective criteria. Others include more subjective criteria. Such criteria may even include reserving a percentage of the final grade for raising a student's grade based on a completely subjective evaluation of the student's level of effort and progress. In no case should such a subjective criterion lower the grade achieved by more objective measures of learning. Grading papers and projects can be particularly difficult. Differentiating between excellent, good, acceptable, and unsatisfactory papers is usually easy; specifying why papers fall in the various categories is much harder.

Over time, the professor develops a set of questions of various types that can be used for quizzes, tests, and examinations. The professor also develops a "feel" for what is reasonable to expect from the average student in a course.

Many students are interested to learn, after a test, how many in the class received A's, B's, etc. and which questions the class as a whole had problems with. Students may submit self-addressed, stamped postcards with final examinations for notification of grades before official transcripts are sent.

The awarding of academic honors at graduation and the election to academic societies such as Phi Beta Kappa and discipline-related societies are based on the grades the student receives for his or her course work.

COMMONLY EVALUATED
ASPECTS OF STUDENT PERFORMANCE

IN-CLASS WORK

Student participation in class provides many opportunities for both formal and informal evaluation. Discussion, group work, individual exercises and written work can all provide data useful in evaluation. The professor may find that work written in class is useful in validating student assignments, papers, and projects prepared out of class.

The professor should be careful to consider the personality of each student in evaluating student participation in class discussions. Some students are simply too shy or too insecure to participate in group discussions. However, these students may be absorbing just as much course-related information as the more talkative student.

OUT-OF-CLASS ASSIGNMENTS

Out-of-class assignments can be used to assess incremental progress in achieving performance objectives. The assignments can provide useful feedback to the professor for clarifying course material, refining ideas, and correcting misperceptions. Feedback from the professor to student on out-of-class assignments gives the student an idea of how he or she is doing in the course and where improvement and more concentrated study is required. There are so many different types of out-of-class assignments that providing guidelines for their evaluation is impossible. In addition to the multitude of types of assignments, evaluation depends on the purpose of the assignment and the weight the professor gives various assignments in the grading policy stated in the syllabus.

LABORATORY WORK

At the undergraduate level, laboratory work is usually highly structured and supervised on a small-group basis. The professor or a laboratory assistant usually has the opportunity to assess the student and his or her work as it is being done. This work can be further evaluated using the laboratory reports and notebooks which the student prepares as formal documentation of the lab experience involving problem solving, experimentation, observation, etc.

Some labs include discussion sections. These discussion sections may be evaluated in much the same way as in-class work is evaluated.

PAPERS AND PROJECTS

Papers and projects form a part of most undergraduate courses. They provide an opportunity to assess higher levels of cognitive and affective learning by providing a way to apply and/or extend classroom learning to a relevant piece of research or practical application. They may be in-depth studies of specific aspects of the course; they may provide the opportunity to accomplish practical work in a subject area; they may reflect individual creative work. In some form or other, they are appropriate for every field of knowledge.

Papers, by definition, are written works. However, most projects require some form of written documentation; therefore, this section treats papers and projects together. Even though a group of students may all work on one project, usually one student is responsible for writing the report or paper which documents the problem, the methodology, and the results of the project. While a paper may only focus on "what the literature says" and be strictly a library-related assignment, a project usually involves learning by doing and often requires searching the literature for related or background information which is included in the documentation for the project.

EVALUATION OF PAPERS:—

The experience of doing a paper can in itself be a learning experience. Papers may represent applications of in-class learning, in-depth studies of specific aspects of the material, or "doing" of the particular subject area. They may reflect individual creative work.

The professor should differentiate in his own mind whether the purpose for the paper is to have the student use the paper-writing experience as a vehicle for dealing with and learning the subject or whether the goal is to have the student learn how to write a paper. Frequently the assignment has a dual purpose. In either case, the professor should make sure that learning is taking place during the experience rather than waiting until the final paper is turned in, for better or worse. Multiple written assignments or short papers may be used. A single term-paper is frequent. In the case of term papers, the professor usually monitors the following aspects:

- Topic choice
- Starting bibliography
- Literature annotations or abstracts
- General outline
- Initial draft.

In topic choice, a list of potential topics is often handed out. Alternatively, students are asked to turn in their topic choices by a given date. The professor may wish to ensure that the topic choices are appropriate to the course goals. Monitoring the starting bibliographies permits the professor to determine whether the student is on the right track and to suggest other helpful sources. Checking literature annotations or abstracts enables the professor to look at written material and to evaluate whether the student is capturing the pertinent aspects. Checking the general outline gives the professor another opportunity to determine whether the student has thought through the material required for the paper as well as whether the student has organized the paper in a logical fashion. Feedback to the student on an initial draft or drafts enables the student to learn from the writing experience and to follow suggestions about how to improve the paper. Use of these check points (and others) can be optional or obligatory.

Instructions for papers should be as clear as possible. Instructions for long papers, especially term papers, should always be in writing. These instructions should include format (e.g. typed, double-spaced), approximate length (e.g. 20-30 pages), and bibliographic style with examples. When appropriate, the subject matter to be included, analyzed, evaluated, etc., should be specified.

Final evaluation of long papers is perhaps most usefully thought of as being similar to refereeing or reviewing a scholarly contribution to the literature. There are four aspects to evaluation of such papers: (1) minimal criteria, (2) other criteria, (3) feedback, and (4) grading.

The minimal criteria are those expected for all satisfactory papers. They include some of the items in the instructions for authors of journal articles. Others are intended to teach students the norms of scholarship. Commonly used minimal criteria are:

- Follow instructions.
- Use specified format.
- Use Standard American English (or other appropriate language).
- Proof-read, especially when using a spell-checker.
- Employ accepted language mechanics (i.e. topic sentences, accurate grammar, paragraphing, etc.).
- Employ consistent and accurate bibliographic form.
- Submit the paper on time.

With regard to timeliness of submission, the following story is instructive. An employee was two weeks late with a report; the firm sustained a $10,000 penalty. The employee was fired.

The professor should also specify the other criteria that will be used to evaluate the paper. These are necessarily more subjective, requiring professional judgment. Such judgments prepare the student for later judgment by his or her peers and superiors. Among the other criteria that may be used, the following are common:

- Knowledge of subject matter
- Coverage of topic—breadth and/or depth
- Originality
- Data Presentation
- Logic
- Organization
- Reasoning
- Analysis
- Synthesis
- Evaluation
- Appropriateness
- Explanation
- Interpretation
- Extrapolation

- Methodology
- Use of the literature
- Scope
- Depth of scholarship
- Accuracy
- Development of themes and/or topics
- Clarity and style of writing

Generally, not more than four or five such criteria are specified, usually those criteria most relevant to the subject matter or the purpose of the paper.

Each student should be given feedback not only on how well he or she has done, but also on how to do better if there were time to revise the paper. Students can learn both from doing the paper and from receiving comments on how to do the next one better. The desirability of giving such feedback must be balanced against the reality of the time available. The professor receives a whole set of papers at the same time and needs to return them quickly, causing time pressures or conflicts with other aspects of his work or with assignments that must be evaluated from other courses.

The use of minimal and other stated criteria for grading papers makes differentiation easier. Students should not be unduly penalized for unsatisfactory aspects of minimal criteria (e.g. for spelling errors) when they have performed well on other stated criteria. Although it is tempting to overuse the minimal criteria because they are more objective, satisfactory minimal criteria should not in themselves be sufficient for good to excellent performance evaluation. Good and excellent performance are graded on the basis of other criteria selected (e.g. from the list above) for evaluating the paper.

Occasionally, a student will turn in a really outstanding paper. Such a paper may be a potential contribution to the professional literature. In these cases, the professor may suggest an appropriate journal and help the student prepare the paper for submission.

An occasional doubtful paper may require that the professor obtain a colleague as a second reader. The professor may wish to retain a copy of the doubtful paper, with his feedback, on file. At times the professor may not be able to determine whether a student has actually written the paper.

EVALUATION OF PROJECTS:—

Projects are often carried out by a group of students. Assigning students to groups has several pitfalls for the unwary professor. The professor must communicate the evaluative criteria he will use at the time the project is assigned. The group needs to know if it will be evaluated as a single entity or if individual contributions to the group will be evaluated. Should the professor decide to evaluate the group as a single entity, he should also be prepared for an outcry from the student who does the most work and who will complain that other group members did not contribute in an equal fashion. While this method reflects "the real world," in the academic environment it does not fairly achieve the academic objective of evaluating individual knowledge gained from the project.

Evaluating each individual in the professor-assigned group can be done in at least two ways. First, each group member can be tested about the project. The leader's knowledge will be obvious, the non-contributor will not test well. This individual testing is rarely satisfactory, especially if it takes up valuable class time. A second, better way, lets each group member evaluate every other group member's performance. This method evaluates effort, but does not necessarily evaluate learning.

Evaluation of group projects becomes much simpler when the group self-selects its own members, knowing from the outset that the group will be evaluated as a single entity. Student self-selection puts responsibility for effort squarely on the group and removes it from the professor.

Project instructions should be as specific as possible. Since instructions will be a criterion for evaluation, they should always be in writing. Written instructions are also useful to the student as a guideline during work on the project. Instructions will vary depending on whether the assignment is a group or an individual effort. In general, the students should know the objective to be achieved by the project, the topic(s) to be addressed, and/or the problem(s) to be solved. Students should also know the minimal acceptable standards for the project in terms of form, materials, due date, etc. The professor's criteria for evaluating the project should, also be included in the written instructions.

INDEPENDENT STUDIES

An independent study is usually a course taken for credit which is individually designed to satisfy a student's particular interest. This interest and the independent study designed to accommodate it are generally assumed to be sufficiently unique that the college would not offer a program course covering the topic of study. In some cases, independent study is part of a course; however, in these cases the independent study is usually a research paper or project having a relatively small scope. Independent study, as defined for this book, refers to the approach to learning used to encourage a close working relationship between a student and a faculty member to develop a highly individualized, rigorous, and personal learning experience.

When the independent study results in a research paper or a project, the product should be evaluated in the same way as any paper or project. Evaluative criteria for independent studies differ from one subject area or project to another. The student and the professor are well advised to agree on the evaluative criteria at the beginning of an independent study. They can then discuss at the end of the study how well the agreed upon criteria have been met.

INTERNSHIPS AND CO-OP PROGRAMS

EVALUATION OF INTERNSHIPS:—

Many colleges and universities give credit for work in a place of employment where the student is involved in tasks related to the student's major. With the increasing demand for job and/or career-related experience by employers, well-chosen and well-supervised internships have become a valuable supplement to the academic experience. Internships vary. Some colleges give academic credit for them, others do not. Some internships pay the student for his or her work, others do not. More important to the evaluative process, though, is the quality and academic relevance of the work which the employer assigns to the intern. Equally important to the evaluative process is the supervision of the intern by the employer and the employer's communication of the student's performance to his or her professorial counterpart. To insure that the student is obtaining the information about how his or her work appears to others, both employer and professor should discuss evaluation with the student during the internship and at its end.

Careful screening of the internship environment and detailed planning of the intern's tasks and assignments before contracting for an internship usually results in a more accurate evaluation of the student's performance.

EVALUATION OF CO-OP PROGRAMS:—

A co-op program provides a student with regularly-scheduled paid work experience as part of his or her academic program. Unlike an internship where a student may be taking courses at the same time as he or she is working as an intern, a co-op program usually implies a full-time job for an entire academic term. Colleges and universities sponsoring co-op programs for their students generally require the student to spend an extra term and/or an extra year to complete their degree. Co-op programs are usually part of an undergraduate experience. The student should know how well he or she is doing. As a part of the experience, it is desirable for the student to receive the same evaluation as a new employee. Opportunities vary for the college to participate in this assessment.

COMPASSIONATE COUNTERPOINTS

Student problems—often beyond their control—mandate the need for some compassionate alternatives to a rigid evaluation system. One of these problems, that of poor test-taking, was discussed in the preceding section on grading. The most effective way to deal with these problems is to anticipate them. A major problem, especially for the first-time professor, is the student tendency to abuse professorial compassion. For instance, the professor soon learns that students are, at times more creative in dreaming up "legitimate" excuses than they are in applying the same creativity to their course work. Grandmothers die regularly. The number of breakdowns which students claim for their cars would overwhelm insurance company statistics. Personal illness or caring for an ill "significant other" seems to happen more often when a project is due than at any other time during the term. The compassionate professor develops a second sense, over time, to distinguish between a real student problem and a contrived excuse. In the meantime, a policy stated in the syllabus to cover the general problems of turning in late assignments, requests for make-up tests and exams, and requests for an "incomplete" instead of a failing grade for uncompleted course work can prevent arguments about many commonly encountered difficulties. Such a policy also generates a sense among students that the professor will be fair to everyone in the class.

LATE ASSIGNMENTS

Because the majority of students are conscientious and will often burn the midnight oil or catch an all-nighter, assignments turned in late should be penalized by a significant reduction in grade. The amount of this reduction is a professorial prerogative, often determined by the importance of the assignment. As a general policy, reducing the evaluation by a full grade point is common.

Extenuating circumstances will sometimes cause this policy to be suspended, but, not surprisingly, the promise of a significant reduction in grade often causes students to pre-plan carefully to complete an assignment early to avoid the grade reduction.

In explaining this policy to students, the professor can also describe his own time constraints and the other commitments which would make evaluating late assignments difficult and detrimental to the students' best interests. The need to evaluate a late assignment can work to a student's disadvantage when the professor has to make extra non-allocated time and may not precisely recall the class norm for the assignment.

MAKE-UP TESTS

Students who are uncertain of their grasp of the course material often find an excuse for a make-up test. This allows the student to ask friends and classmates about the test and gain an unfair advantage over other students who do not have prior knowledge.

The easiest policy to enforce is avoidance. Do not give make-up tests. The student who cannot take the test on the date specified is given a failing grade. This policy assumes that the dates for tests are given to the student at the beginning of the term, allowing the student to plan his or her own schedule.

Modifications to this policy often are needed, especially during the mid-term exam period, when a large group of students may have an unreasonable number of tests scheduled for one day. Then the compassionate professor can reschedule the test date and still implement the no make-up policy.

EXTRA CREDIT

Students generally request an extra-credit assignment to overcome an unsatisfactory grade level in a course. Such a request has two implications, one for the professor and one for the student. The professor is taking on extra work in making the assignment, monitoring its progress, and evaluating the finished product. The student is also taking on extra work in a course where present efforts have not resulted in a satisfactory grade level. Both the professor and the student must address the value of such extra-credit assignments in light of the extra work created.

Extra-credit work is to be encouraged for the bright student wishing to go beyond the requirements of the course. Many professors enjoy helping a motivated student pursue an area in which the student has shown a real interest. Both the student and the professor benefit from this type of extra-credit assignment.

INCOMPLETE GRADES

Most college and university grading policies allow a professor to give a student an incomplete grade for a course as an alternative to a failing grade when satisfactory work has been completed for at least two-thirds of the course. The course work is generally expected to be completed by the end of the term following the incomplete grade.

Many valid reasons can be cited for giving an "incomplete." These reasons can be personal and/or academic. A death or divorce in the family can cause major upheavals for a student, making it impossible to continue to do satisfactory work in the course. Students do succumb to serious illnesses which prevent their completing course work. Often a valid project turns out to be more time-consuming than the professor intended or the student realized, yet both student and professor wish to see the project completed. The bibliographic materials necessary for a research paper may have arrived too late making a thoroughly investigated paper impossible to write. Each of these reasons would merit an incomplete rather than a failing grade.

Chapter 11

DEVELOPING AS A
LEARNING MANAGER

Colleges and universities are paying increasing attention to faculty development. Learning management involves keeping up with developments in the field, improving teaching skills, revising courses, and developing new courses. Effective use of both teaching- and student-support services is important. Planning and designing courses (Chapter 4) is distinguished from the preparation for learning management discussed in this chapter. Preparation is the continuing process of developing as a learning manager.

The professor teaching an "established" course for the first time sometimes can follow a previously designed outline or syllabus. The course can be revised when the professor teaches the course for the second time and in subsequent terms. The professor's continuing education and monitoring of progress in her subject area will lead to course revision. From time to time, curriculum revision and developments in a program area may lead the professor to prepare a completely new course not previously offered by the college or university. The revising of an "established" course and the preparation of a new course are part of the professor's development as a learning manager.

The professor's first term in a new college or university may be so taken up with learning the ropes and becoming acquainted with the general characteristics of the student body that she has little time to become well acquainted with the various teaching support services provided by the institution. Even to teach "established" courses, the professor will find the support services offered by the college or university of immeasurable value. When revising a course, and especially when preparing a new course, the professor will find these support services invaluable. These services can also be of help in keeping up with the professor's subject field and in her own research.

The topics of initial preparation, ongoing preparation, course revision, continuing education, preparation of new courses, use of support services, and learning about teaching are important to the development of the professor as a learning manager. This chapter discusses each of them.

INITIAL PREPARATION

The new professor is expected to be prepared to step in and teach established courses. Those professors who have time before the beginning of the term might consider the recommendations under Course Revision later in this chapter. The professor who is pressed for time can plan as indicated in Chapter 4. Many institutions have an orientation day for new faculty which includes an introduction to the various student and faculty support services. In addition, the following ideas and suggestions for initial preparation may be helpful.

Previous education and experience are the main sources of ideas for beginning teaching. Spending time thinking about the topics that will be covered in each course and their sequence is important. Alternative methods of teaching should also be considered. Lectures are not the only method of presenting subject material. Unfortunately, reading about different methods of presentation is often dull or limited to "how-I-did-it-good." The professor may prefer to consult friends and colleagues and to think about which methods she might find most comfortable and effective. In addition to considering methods of teaching, the professor should also consider methods of evaluating student learning, selecting those which will be most meaningful for the students in the context of the goals and objectives' for the course.

ONGOING PREPARATION

Ongoing preparation depends on keeping up with the field or subject area. The college or university professor faces a dual problem in keeping up with her field: the demands of managing student learning in several courses and the demands of her own interests in research and publication. The demands for participation in college and university committee work and student and community activities also add to the problem of keeping up.

A professor, without the responsibility for communicating to first- and second-year undergraduates, may become so narrowly focused on her field that she cannot forge the relevant links between her own expertise and the broader areas of the students' limited experience. In keeping up with the field, some breadth of current general information is as vital to the success of managing student learning as current expertise in a narrower subject area.

Keeping Up

For all professors, especially those not working intensively at the cutting edge of a research area, the amount of study necessary to keep up with general knowledge, to say nothing of their own subject area, is overwhelming. For some time, the amount of recorded scholarly information has been doubling every seven to ten years. This means that the amount of information published in the last ten years is as great as all of the information previously published in history. Concomitant with this information explosion, or perhaps a cause of it, is the increased specialization in so many areas. As a result, scholars in the same basic discipline but working in different subfields may have difficulties understanding both the language and the literature of their highly specialized colleagues.

To keep up with information in print, the college or university professor usually subscribes to journals and scans others in the library. Articles of interest to colleagues can be photocopied and circulated to provide a common knowledge base within a departmental program. Articles or books reviewing the developments and activities in a specialized area are particularly useful. These review publications serve as summaries, providing an overview or perspective of an area with which the professor may not be very familiar or current. The use of online bibliographic databases offers the means to generate relevant references quickly for either retrospective or current interests. Reference and subject specialist librarians can assist the professor in keeping up with new information.

Miscellaneous Sources of Ideas and Information

Many ideas arise from a variety of miscellaneous sources. The professor's own research findings are obvious sources, as is consulting. Other ideas arise in the course of everyday life. Non-professional reading, television viewing, politics, community contacts, entertainment, and even everyday life are sources of issues and information that lend contemporary relevance to teaching as learning management.

Contacts with Colleagues

Many ideas come from colleagues within the department, the college or university, or other places of work. Meetings are an important source of current information and of face-to-face conversation with geographically scattered colleagues sharing similar research and subject area interests. Although many large meetings publish in their proceedings all the papers given (at least in abstract form), the professor derives the most benefit from the opportunity meetings afford for informal discussions with colleagues sharing similar interests. Cooperative research projects develop from such discussions. New approaches to teaching a subject of common interest can also be learned. Well-known researchers presenting their papers can be asked questions directly during discussion periods. The professor's own research can be offered for informal criticism to her colleagues. Most professors aim to attend at least one major professional society meeting each year.

Continuing Education Courses

Many colleges and universities, as well as commercial enterprises, offer continuing education courses. Many professional societies offer courses in new and specialized areas, often before or after a general conference. These courses enable college and university professors, as well as other interested persons, to continue their education and to keep up with new developments in a subject area. Some professional societies require that members earn continuing education credits by taking society-sponsored courses to maintain professional status or licenses.

Vacations and Sabbaticals

Professors, like everyone else, need vacations. The time away from teaching (whether as a vacation, a sabbatical or a leave of absence), provides time for the reading in depth, thinking at length, and writing that are difficult within the time constraints of the regular semester. Professors also need time to visit various sites important to their teaching subject. The professor who teaches the 19th century English novel must have time to go to England to absorb the ambience. The archaeologist must have time to go on a dig, the Russian historian to the USSR, and so forth. Vacations allow time to explore distant museums and libraries. Often they are the time for scholarly research.

Travel frequently provides opportunities to take photographic slides to be used in the classroom. Vacations may be used to develop new courses and to revise old ones. Rest and relaxation are needed for rejuvenation.

In addition to vacations, other respites from teaching enable the professor to keep up to date in her field and are sources of ideas and information. Tenured professors can request sabbatical leave for specific scholarly or research purposes. Faculty are sometimes "loaned" for government service or to industry for a specific period of time. Exchange teaching enables a professor to teach in another college or university as a "visiting professor." Time away from one's own academic institution can be productive for the professor, her students, and the institution itself.

COURSE REVISION

Each time the professor offers a course, unless it is completely "canned," she begins a new and exciting experiment. The interactions between the professor and the individual students in a class, even with material that has not been changed for several terms, result in learning which cannot be completely predetermined. Most professors assess the results, in this ongoing experiment, at the end of each term. This assessment can be a result of self-evaluation or student evaluations. The assessment can continue throughout the term. Following these assessments, the professor may wish to try new approaches to presenting course materials the next time she offers the course. The professor should add or remove material from the course in the light of new knowledge in the subject being taught.

Gathering Information for Course Revision

Keeping a separate file and/or set of folders containing information about course revision makes the process much easier to implement. Information can be placed in the file or folders on an ongoing, systematic basis. Drop informal notes in the file about which approaches to learning management are most successful and which approaches should be dropped or discarded. Also add notes, articles, and clippings providing ideas about new approaches which might be worth incorporating in the future.

Gather current reading that applies to each class session. Photocopy relevant articles about changes, advances, or new developments in the subject area. Photocopy or take notes about any interesting ideas for activities that would develop student interest in and knowledge of the subject. Keep a list of new and current books and audiovisual and/or computerized instructional materials on the subject. Request examination copies of new textbooks.

Focus on student reactions to the course. Consider the background of students who took the course. Would a greater understanding of student backgrounds have changed course goals and objectives, course content, or methods of presenting the learning materials? What information was learned from student evaluations of the course? Were any criticism or suggestions well-founded? If so, how could the course be revised for the next class to benefit from the criticism or suggestions?

Each time the professor teaches the same course, the information gathered for course revision can be used to improve the course design and to manage student learning more effectively.

Implementing Course Revision

The following steps can help the professor to make course revision more systematic and efficient:

1) Review the course goals and objectives. Were they achieved as indicated by the professor's self-evaluation and by the students' achievement and evaluation of the course? If not, how could they be modified to meet student needs while fitting into the total curricular structure of the departmental program?

2) Select from the file and/or folders any new information that should be included in the course. Also consider any different activities which might be added, as well as any information or activities which should be removed. Consider the possibility of adopting a new text for the course based on the evaluation of newly published or discovered texts which cover the course content and reflect the course goals and objectives.

3) Revise the course design and the syllabus to reflect new information and any modification of goals, objectives, new materials, different activities.

4) Submit the revised course syllabus to be typed (if necessary) and reproduced *well in advance* of the first day of the course. Typing and reprographic services are usually overwhelmed at the beginning of the term and have been known to make tardy professors wait for several days into the course before the class can benefit from the syllabus.

5) Deposit the syllabus in the departmental or library files as required by institutional policy.

6) Review notes and lesson plans before each class session for a well-organized presentation of information and activities.

The first time the professor teaches a course, whether the course has been "established" by a colleague or newly prepared, is rarely a satisfactory experience. The nature of the impossible-to-quantify variables in the teaching experiment plus the lack of experiential data make success the first time around more a matter of luck than of expertise. The second time the professor teaches the same course, more data are available on the background of students interested in the course and on their reactions to the materials and activities.

PREPARATION OF NEW COURSES

New courses usually need to go through some type of approval process. They may need to pass through various curriculum committees and through various levels in the college or university. Sometimes the professor is asked to develop a new course, and sometimes she wishes to suggest one because of personal or perceived student interest or because of significant new developments in a discipline. Usually a one-page outline of the content is sufficient for the various curriculum committees and levels of administration. The relationship of the proposed new course to other existing courses, as well as any prerequisites for the course, may be requested.

When a new course is initially designed, its relationship to the rest of the curriculum or departmental program must be considered. What level of student will be taking the course? Will the course be one required for graduation in the major? Will any prerequisites be required? Will the course be a prerequisite to others? The professor should know the course content of related courses within the department as well as in other areas of the college or university. The new course should complement and reinforce the importance of related courses without overlapping their subject content.

General Preparation

The goals and objectives of the course should be determined before any other specific preparation is begun. In determining goals and objectives, the professor may wish to consider some broad philosophical considerations as well as specific departmental goals for the course. The philosophical considerations may include whether the learning to be accomplished will enable students to be informed citizens, to be prepared for specific occupational areas, or to be capable of life-long learning in the subject.

General preparation should include the following tasks:

• Defining the scope of the course in light of its goals and objectives and the length of the term;

• Defining the level of the students who will be taking the course;

• Determining prerequisite courses that students will be expected to have completed and/or prior knowledge and skills that will be expected of the students taking the course;

• Investigating available textbooks and other teaching materials available for purchase;

• Investigating library and media center resources to support the course and student independent study necessary for learning course content. This investigation might result in a list of supplemental materials for students to pursue;

• Deciding on the most effective method(s) of presenting course content;

• Investigating computer center resources for suggestions;

• Deciding whether the goals and objectives require the use of laboratory periods and, if so, what kind;

• Deciding what assignments will be most effective for learning;

• Deciding on the evaluative methods to be used.

Specific Preparations

Textbook selection is one of the most important tasks in preparing for a new course. For courses where one or more textbooks form the basis of the course, texts are usually selected either by an individual professor (one who has the primary responsibility for the course) or by a committee. In most colleges and universities, the various sections of one course generally use the same text to insure consistency of learning. This consistency is especially helpful when a course with various sections is a prerequisite for a more advanced course.

Regardless of whether texts are selected by a single individual or by committee, a professor interested in keeping up to date in the field will wish to stay abreast of new texts published in the area of her teaching. Publishers will frequently send interested faculty copies of new texts to review for possible course adoption. In recent years this practice has been severely curtailed. Textbook publication costs are very high and the market for most texts is limited. Furthermore, too many professors have taken advantage of publishers' generosity to build their own professional libraries at the publishers' expense.

Unless an adoption order follows or the review copy is returned in a timely manner, the publisher may charge the professor for the text.

Once a text is selected, the professor must decide how closely to follow the text. Clearly, if the only course learning is to come from the text, the student will have little reason for enrolling in a course except to gain needed credits for graduation. A skillful professor will supplement the text with her own experience and with additional materials from the library or from personal files.

When reviewing a textbook for possible adoption, the professor will want to consider several factors:

1) How well does the text meet course objectives?

2) Does the text adequately cover the course content?

3) Is the text up to date and written at a level students can understand?

4) Will the text be suitable for adjunct faculty use or for other full-time faculty teaching additional course sections?

5) Does the text contain practice exercises, authoritative and up-to-date bibliography, notes, glossary, etc?

6) Does the author provide a teachers' guide, test banks, computer data disks, slides for overhead projection?

7) Are items 5 and 6 desirable and/or necessary for a suitable text for this course?

8) Is the cost in line with other texts having a similar value?

9) Is the text useful only for this course or can the student use it in other courses or after graduation?

Selection of supplementary and suggested readings usually occurs once the textbook is selected. Few texts are adequate to convey all the information within the scope of a specific course. Furthermore, the textbook gives only one author's ideas and perspective on a subject.

The supplementary readings should be included in the course syllabus and made easily accessible to the student. One way of making supplementary readings accessible is to put them on the reserve reading shelf in the library. The suggested reading list should be kept relatively short. Readings on this list should be available in the general library collection or through inter-library loan.

Media and equipment selection will supplement the text selected for the course. Media and equipment may also be used instead of a textbook, especially in new areas of knowledge where an authoritative textbook has yet to be published. Some equipment may be used only by the professor. Other equipment may be required of the students taking the course. Art supplies and computer diskettes are good examples of equipment often needed by students taking a course.

Reading a textbook and listening to a professor's lectures are only two channels of many through which students learn. In today's multimedia world, the professor has a wide array of educational media which she can use to augment and reinforce a textbook-based lecture.

Careful review is required before selecting any piece of media. The professor must also ask herself several questions:

1) Is the content relevant to the course objectives?

2) Is the presentation clear?

3) How will this media add to or reinforce the information that I wish to communicate to my students?

4) How easily can I obtain this additional media?

5) What kind of equipment will I need to use with this media?

6) Can I operate this equipment without difficulty?

7) What backup means of instruction do I have should the media (or the equipment needed for it) malfunction? Murphy's Law tends to operate with more than usual regularity when using supplemental media and accompanying equipment in a classroom situation.

In addition to these questions, the professor must also consider the possibility that students may have seen a particular movie or filmstrip or have heard a particular audiotape, etc. in another course. Repetition of the same media selection in more than one course is a frequent cause of student boredom and inattention, even when the learning objectives are different. Rather than repeat the media selection, the professor should plan to save time by simply referring to the particular selection to make the instructional point. An assignment to view, listen to, or use that particular media selection can be made for those students not familiar with it.

Even in a college or university whose library has an excellent media and equipment collection, the professor will often need a selection which the library's collection does not own. In such cases, the library will often be able to obtain this selection on inter-library loan or be able to rent the needed selection. Whether the selection can be obtained on loan or by rental, the professor should make this request to the library as soon as possible—even before the term begins—to insure that it can be obtained and that the request falls within the library's budgetary guidelines.

Develop the syllabus for the course as described in Chapter 4: Course Planning and Design. Have the syllabus reproduced for discussion and comments from colleagues in the department or program.

Arrange the use of reserve materials with the library and, if appropriate, give the library a copy of the syllabus with any additional required or suggested readings not placed on the reserve reading shelves. The library should also be made aware of any assignments which will utilize special subject areas of its collection.

Design and produce any custom materials necessary for classroom instruction. In some colleges and universities, the graphics department will assist with this task. In other colleges, the professor must design and produce any custom materials by herself.

Preparation for Individual Classroom Sessions

Once the general and specific preparations for a new course have been accomplished, a set of classroom session folders will enable the course to proceed more smoothly the first time it is offered. This final level of preparation also insures that the course will not get "off track" and will accomplish those goals and objectives for which it was designed. Preparing for individual classroom sessions before the term begins will enable the inevitable adjustments in the course to be made easily and quickly. The professor will save much valuable time.

The folders for each session might contain the following information and materials:

• Objectives for the session.

• Material(s) required for the session. These may include lecture notes, questions for discussion, personal slides and/or transparencies, a list of other equipment and/or media to be supplied by the media department, outside assignments, review and test questions, etc.

• Outline for the session. This includes a review of the previous class session as well as the major points to be covered in the session and the methods used to make these points.

Time allocations for various classroom activities may also be included.

USE OF SUPPORT SERVICES

Teaching Support Services

Developing good relationships with the personnel in various teaching support services is well worth the time invested. These people are essential when support is needed. Secretarial services, student assistants, the library-media center, and the computer center all provide support to make the professor's teaching more effective. Developing as a learning manager requires the professor to make optimal use of student advisory and support services.

Secretarial Services

Many colleges and universities have a secretarial pool to assist the professor with typing, reproducing syllabi, taking messages, scheduling, etc. One secretary may serve as office manager or as administrative assistant to a dean or department chairman. The office manager/administrative assistant will assist the new professor by acquainting her with the secretarial services available.

Library and Media Center

In many colleges and universities the library and the media center are combined as one administrative unit to provide supplemental materials and research information for students and faculty. The library traditionally has housed the print-oriented information and the media center has been responsible for non-print media and its associated equipment. As this distinction has become blurred with the use of computerized databases for locating and retrieving print information, catalogs which combine print and non-print holdings, as well as compact optical disks for storing and retrieving print information, the use of the term "library" has become generic. Some colleges now use the term "resource center" to more accurately describe an integrated print and non-print facility. For purposes of this book, the term "library" will be used to mean the central information resource center supporting teaching and learning, regardless of the form of information contained in the center.

Subject-specialist librarians will be familiar with publication announcements and reviews of books. They may suggest new or related material for courses. Librarians know the structure of the collection and how to locate material in the institution's library system and other libraries and archives. They can be helpful in arranging visits to special collections. Frequently, one or more librarians specializes in media. For example, a film librarian will be familiar with sources of films and reviews of films. An art librarian may be in charge of a slide collection. A documents librarian in charge of government reports will be able to locate copies of legislation and copies of government-funded research reports.

To become familiar with available course material, the knowledgeable professor becomes closely acquainted with the library and its staff as soon as possible. Supplemental resources are invaluable to motivate and expand the knowledge of the brilliant student beyond the stated course content. Should the library not own certain materials which the faculty would use on a regular basis, the librarian responsible for acquisitions should be alerted to order or rent these materials. Inter-library loan can be used to obtain needed information quickly, particularly with the increasing use of telefacsimile machines.

The library will also place specified material on reserve for student use. This insures that the reserved materials will be equally accessible to all students for a limited period of time. Students may complain about the inconvenience of having to spend time in the library to use or to take out reserve materials. However, it is important for students to learn to use the library effectively.

Since the library usually includes instruction-in-use as one of its major services to incoming students, faculty often assume that students know how to gain access to the many resources and services which the library offers. Some faculty, though, take advantage of the library's instructional services to show a class the specific informational materials which are available to supplement their texts and to locate information for term papers and projects.

Students are not the only ones who can take advantage of the library's services for their research. Even the smallest college has access to a wealth of scholarly material. The computerized online databases provide immediate access to abstracts of millions of research reports and papers. Obtaining an entire report or paper has become a simple matter of requesting the report and, depending on institutional policy, paying for it. Computerized telecommunication has provided libraries with instant access to more information than any one library could possibly hold within its own walls. The ability to gain access to this information is the test of a skilled, professional librarian and one of the most valuable services which today's library provides to teaching and research faculty.

Computer Center

In its instructional role, the computer center supports the faculty by providing assistance with the use of computers for learning in many areas such as:

1) writing with word-processing packages;

2) assisting drill and practice instruction with a computer-assisted instruction package;

3) designing copy with desk-top publishing packages;

4) solving a scientific or mathematical problem with an appropriate programming language;

5) designing a database with a database application package;

6) designing a piece of equipment with a computer-aided design application package;

7) setting up an accounting or financial system with an appropriate spread-sheet or database application package;

8) evaluating a specified system with a computer-assisted system evaluation application package.

A large university with a well-equipped computer center and a graduate program in engineering or computer science will also provide faculty support to students learning to construct a computer and for research in improving current computing technology. University computer centers are currently involved in parallel processing and artificial intelligence. The computing facilities of a small college are often limited to helping students learn one or more programming languages and one or more application packages as detailed above.

Student Assistants

Student assistants can be very helpful in doing such tasks as online searching, chasing down sources, checking bibliographies and reading lists, proofreading and copy editing, assisting with manuscript preparation, helping with the preparation of slides and other visual aids, ordering books, and attending to routine correspondence. Some professors have learned that sending the student assistant to search the literature results in the assistant knowing the literature better than the professor. If the search is to identify one or more known items, having the student assistant locate the item is very helpful. However, becoming familiar with what is written and who has done the writing is a different issue. Some professors and administrators feel strongly that student assistants should not be given clerical tasks. Yet, it is the rare professor who has never sent a student to photocopy an article.

Many professors feel strongly that students should *not* be used to grade their fellow students. This is particularly true when the assistant is at the same level or has not taken the course. Others feel that a third-year student can be taught to grade first-year courses. Clearly, there is a difference between having a student assistant score objective tests and using the assistant to write evaluative comments on essay exams or papers. Students have been used very successfully in Personalized Systems of Instruction (see Chapter 6: Laboratory Learning). Ultimately, the responsibility for grading belongs to the professor. Guiding teaching assistants, research assistants, and laboratory assistants is discussed in Chapter 9: Mentoring and Other Ways of Interacting with Students.

The department chairman or dean is the person that the professor should contact about acquiring a student assistant. The number of hours per week which a student assistant works will vary with the size of the college's work-study program and the number of professors who need student assistants.

Student Advisory and Support Services

All campuses have many services available to assist students. Professors need to be aware of these in order to be prepared to make referrals as needed. Among these services are the following:

Academic Advising - An administrative function in many colleges and universities. Academic advisors know course sequences, prerequisites and the times when a course is offered. They can help in registration for courses; they usually check on incomplete grades and may deal with withdrawals. Usually they do not substitute for the professor in giving specific career advice.

Career Centers - May arrange for interest testing and job interviews. They have sources of career material, brochures, announcements of job openings, graduate school catalogs, and information about admissions tests. They may also house files with student transcripts and faculty recommendations. Writing recommendations to be placed in the student's career center file saves the professor from being asked to respond to each prospective employer or graduate school separately.

Counseling Services - Help with adjustment and personal problems.

Medical Service - Deals with student health.

Chaplaincy Service - Arranges for religious services and fellowship in addition to counseling in matters of faith and morals.

Study Skills Center - Arranges help with study skills, tutorials and remediation.

Foreign Student Advisors - Assist in adjustment to the academic and to the local community. Help with problems of scholarships and visas.

These centers are staffed with skilled professionals. Professors should refer students to these centers whenever mentoring goes beyond their own time or competence. The professor who is familiar with one or more staff members at these centers is better prepared to make such referrals.

LEARNING MORE ABOUT TEACHING

Academia is putting increasing emphasis on faculty development. Some campuses now have instructional development centers with personnel available to assist in developing courseware, particularly courseware that uses technology. Some institutions provide assistance in improvement and self-evaluation. This assistance may include opportunities for the professor to videotape herself giving a lecture.

Faculty retreats can be used to discuss teaching. Workshops on teaching methods are increasingly prevalent.

● ● ● ● ● ● ● ● ● ● ● ● ● ● ●

In summary, preparation for learning management is a continuous process. The excellent professor continues to learn and grow in both the subject field and in the methods of learning management. On-going preparation is one of the hallmarks of the learning manager. Much general preparation occurs in the context of the professor's other responsibilities, which are discussed in Part III.

Part III

The Professor's Varied Roles

Chapter **12**

ACADEMIC FREEDOM AND COLLEGIALITY

The traditions of academic freedom and collegiality explain why teaching, service, and research are the parameters of the professor business. Both academic freedom and collegiality have a long history. The notion of academic freedom first emerged in the German universities of the nineteenth century where it applied to the students' freedom to learn and the professors' freedom in teaching and research. Collegiality emerged from the medieval tradition of a community of scholars living and working together. Both are of great importance in the development of higher education in the United States and are essential to the understanding of academia today.

ACADEMIC FREEDOM

The end of the nineteenth century was a period of increasing specialization within American curricula. Many new disciplines arose and many courses were added to the traditional ones. Programs expanded and universities as we know them today began to develop. Many schools were operated under the auspices of religious organizations. Some received state and federal support. Others were private institutions. Legal responsibility rested in the Boards of these organizations. Because some Boards tried to dictate what professors were to teach and what kind of research was to be conducted, the AAUP (American Association of University Professors) met to determine a response to these restrictions.

By 1915, the AAUP issued a Declaration of Principles which became the basis for academic freedom in the United States. Many colleges and universities subscribed to the Principles. The courts have tended to interpret them as rights protected by the First Amendment. The Principles have been reaffirmed repeatedly since 1915. The Principles (Joughlin) describe the function of the professor as follows:

> That function is to deal at first hand, after prolonged and specialized technical training, with the sources of knowledge; and to impart the results of their own and of their fellow specialists' investigation and reflection, both to students and to the general public, without fear or favor. (p 162)

The Principles tried to clarify the difference between professors in academic organizations and employees of other organizations. Thus, according to the statement, professors are "appointees" (p 165) of the Board of Trustees, but not "employees" (p 163). They are not employees in the sense that they may not be told what to investigate, how to teach, or what to say and do professionally. This independence is essential. The same Principles specify the research, teaching, and service purposes of the college or university as:

"A. To promote inquiry and advance the sum of human knowledge.

B. To provide general instruction to the students.

C. To develop experts for various branches of the public service." (pp 163-164).

They say further that for research: "In all . . . domains of knowledge, the first condition of progress is complete and unlimited freedom to pursue inquiry and publish its results." (p 164) In regard to teaching, the Principles state: "There must be in the mind of the teacher no mental reservation. He must give the student the best of what he had and what he is." (p 165) Finally, both government and industry must be completely confident in the disinterestedness of the professor for him to be able to give the best public service. "The university should be an intellectual experiment station where new ideas may germinate and where their fruit, though still distasteful to the community as a whole, may be allowed to ripen until finally, perchance, it may become a part of the accepted intellectual food of the nation or of the world. Not less is it a distinctive duty of the university to be the conservator of all genuine elements of value in the past thought and life of mankind which are not in the fashion of the moment." (pp 167-168).

In order to promote free inquiry, optimal instruction of students, and experts for public service, it was considered important that professors not be told what to do or think. Partly because of these considerations, reappointment and tenure became an important aspect of the academic system. Tenure prevented professors from being dismissed for holding opinions at variance with the general public view. The principles of academic freedom are an important part of the history and value system within colleges and universities.

COLLEGIALITY

The notion of "college" implies collegiality, i.e., a group of colleagues working together. Collegiality implies using many informal opportunities to share and explore intellectual ideas. It implies learning from each other. Collegiality is the basis of the college atmosphere in all aspects: teaching, service, and research.

Collegiality is of increased importance to teaching today because of the difficulty of keeping up with advances in knowledge. Professors must be aware of what is going on in other areas to integrate the classroom with contemporary scholarship. Many of the newer teaching techniques, especially those involving instructional technology, are the result of group efforts. Courses may be developed cooperatively or in tandem.

The professors retain for themselves the right to decide what goes on in the classroom, in research, and in the curricular offerings or academic program. The faculty undertakes responsibility for the self-governance of the academic programs within the institution. This responsibility entails colleagues meeting together in committees and symposia and sharing decision-making and knowledge.

Collegiality is necessary for developing and discussing new research ideas. Basic research and innovative scholarship is nourished in an atmosphere separated from the pressures of production, mission orientation, product development, or the achievement of a more profitable bottom line. Collegiality facilitates team research in basic areas and is a necessary response to the call for interdisciplinary research. Basic research is the traditional provenance of the university. Such research may have no foreseeable application or commercial product. Therefore it is not appropriate for the research departments of most commercial organizations. These businesses usually focus on applied research. Yet in the sciences, insights from such basic research frequently form the underpinnings many decades later of unimagined new technologies and even whole new industries. Basic research and innovative scholarship in the social sciences, the arts and humanities also develop new theories, insights and understandings that affect human behavior, bodies politic and artistic enjoyment over long time spans.

In the global village which is the world today, collegiality extends beyond the institution. Colleagues work together from different institutions to develop and share learning technology. Multi-institutional committees ensure that accreditation standards are met, come up with standardized subject discipline curricula, and plan conferences and meetings. Multiple site research is increasingly common and findings are shared around the world, often before formal publication. This sharing is facilitated by telecommunication technology.

THE ACADEMY IN SOCIETY

Colleges and universities occupy a unique position in society partly because of academic freedom and partly because of collegiality. The professor functions in several communities: (1) the college or university community; (2) the professional community of his discipline; and (3) the lay community in which he lives. The professor's record of research and publication is indicative of keeping up with a discipline area and infusing classroom teaching with up-to-date information.

The professor's varied roles often require standing apart from one or more of the communities in which he functions to take a longer or different view based on the variety of information to which he is exposed. This ability to stand apart and to speak or write from a different or more objective perspective can only occur in an atmosphere of intellectual freedom and independence. The collegial atmosphere contributes to the unique character of each institution, to alumni loyalty, and to society's view of higher education.

Faculty feel strongly about academic freedom and cherish collegiality. Professors believe that their expertise should determine what should be taught and what research they will pursue. Today, the general public is increasingly calling upon faculty to account for these decisions.

Chapter **13**

THE TEACHING ROLE AND ITS RESPONSIBILITIES

The professor's teaching role includes a variety of responsibilities which have a synergistic relationship to her roles and responsibilities in service, research, and publication. Above all else, the professor must strive for excellence in teaching. However, there are other aspects of teaching in addition to those described as learning management in Part II. The professor must handle the administrative responsibilities involved in documenting student learning and in keeping track of those students who have registered for her courses. The professor must evaluate her teaching and respond to the evaluations of her teaching by students, by peers, and by the administration. The professor must deal with concerns about legal and affirmative action issues. Finally, the professor must be concerned about her own career progress as a teacher. This progress is defined by the level of appointment, promotion, and tenure.

THE RESPONSIBILITY FOR EXCELLENCE

In the current social climate, excellence is an important goal. Excellence in college teaching is no exception. Professors may be experts in their subject areas, but subject expertise does not guarantee teaching expertise. This book gives the professor some tips for teaching, focusing on the student who is the recipient of the professor's teaching. This focus is termed "learning management." The ways of managing the student's learning environment most effectively, particularly in a classroom group, are limited only by the professor's creativity and imagination. Teaching in an environment of academic freedom means that each professor can give her best efforts to each student.

Teaching is difficult to evaluate. Excellent teaching in higher education is particularly difficult to evaluate. Teaching in the liberal arts is probably more difficult to evaluate than professional training. In professional training, specific skills must be developed to work in, for example, computer science or financial management. However, in the liberal arts, the student should be prepared to undertake a wide variety of roles within society, including employment, responsible citizenship, life-long learning, and (perhaps) parenting.

The public at large has general expectancies for college and university graduates. Employers tend to want graduates to be able to step into a job and work with minimal additional training. Yet employers are also concerned with the obsolescence of their employees' job skills. Many firms now provide in-house courses to keep their employees' skills up to date. Teaching and training in industry is a large enterprise which frequently calls upon the expertise of college professors. Industry will also invest in the latest educational technology if it will make learning more effective. Colleges and universities, on the other hand, often have to deal with limited budgets which restrict technological resources.

The pressure and temptation to teach students to step immediately into a job must be balanced against the awareness that economic change and technological obsolescence come quickly. Students must also be prepared for the future. The graduate may change career paths. The graduate should be able to change with the times and not be so specialized that he or she must return for formal schooling each time a job change is wanted or needed.

The exciting developments in educational technology seem to hold much promise for enhancing excellence in learning management. However, sophisticated technology is not always the solution to every learning situation. Many early computer applications for learning focused on drill-and-practice, which is useful, but not very exciting. The use of computers for simulating learning situations continues to develop. The professor will take advantage of developments in educational technology where the developments result in appropriate tools for learning, not simply where the developments are the newest tools.

In striving for excellence in learning management, the professor must balance the various pressures, needs, and values within society and within the college or university against her own values. Institutions of higher education are putting more and more emphasis on the importance of excellence in teaching; however, classroom teaching is only one aspect of the professor's responsibilities.

THE RESPONSIBILITY FOR CLASSROOM ADMINISTRATION

Teaching Load

Each professor is responsible for teaching a specified number of courses each term. This responsibility becomes the professor's teaching load. The number of courses taught will vary from one college or university to another. The number will also vary within a college or university depending on whether the professor is given "released time" (i.e., a lighter teaching load) for administrative assignments or research. Professors may also be asked to assume an "overload," usually for some additional financial compensation. Summer-term teaching, especially for junior faculty, may be required; a separate contract is often provided for teaching outside of the regular academic year.

Meeting Classes

The classroom hours spent teaching are usually called "contact hours." The number of contact hours for a course is related to the requirements for licensing by the state and for approval by the various accrediting bodies. The number of contact hours per course per week is usually equated with the number of credits that the student will receive for the course.

The professor is, of course, expected to meet all scheduled classes. Attendance at professional meetings should be arranged so that students do not have fewer contact hours than specified by the course. The professor can usually arrange for a colleague to be a guest speaker in class while she is away. Most professors struggle into class even when ill, unless the illness is severe. The class can be taught, and the professor can then return to bed. Even the professor coping with a death in the immediate family will attempt to have her class covered. Teaching is the last responsibility to be eliminated.

Make-up classes are difficult to schedule because of institutional demands on classroom space. In addition to these demands, students either have other classes or work obligations which make rescheduling very difficult. An all-day field trip may, for the same reasons, be as difficult to schedule during the week as a make-up class.

Student Attendance in Class

The college or university may state an attendance policy. Otherwise, the professor determines her own attendance policy. At some time in the first few weeks of each term, an attendance sheet may be required by the Registrar. Most colleges and universities also have a period during which a student may withdraw from a course without penalty, or during which a student may withdraw by paying some portion of the course fee. These policies for withdrawal are usually specified in the college catalog.

Students who do not have the background or prerequisite courses for a course should be urged to withdraw before suffering a financial penalty or a failing grade. Failing grades have a negative influence on prospective employers and prospects for admission to graduate programs. They have also been an issue in political campaigns!

Grades

As distasteful as the grading process is to many professors, the professor has a responsibility to students as well as to the college or university to turn in final course grades on time. Colleges vary in their policy for giving students a failing grade or an "incomplete" when the professor does not fulfill this responsibility. The student may suffer real financial hardship should the professor not turn in grades on time. Scholarship awards and renewals are affected, as is reimbursement by employers for successful completion of the course. Lack of a grade may prevent a student from making the Dean's List. Job acceptance and admission to graduate school can also be affected.

The professor must also follow up on grades of "incomplete" she has given to students, even when she accepts a job elsewhere. Rules for resolving a grade of "incomplete" are usually found in the college catalog; however, one common resolution is automatic failure in the course unless the professor otherwise changes the grade.

EVALUATION OF TEACHING

The performance of the professor in each of her varied roles is evaluated for reappointment, promotion, and tenure. Teaching is supposed to be the most important factor in the overall evaluation of a professor's performance. In fact, in many colleges and universities, the professor's performance as a teacher becomes secondary to the professor's record of research and publication. The professor beginning her career should be aware that this discrepancy between the stated weight of teaching and the actual weight of research does exist, especially in promotion and tenure decisions made at the administrative level.

Student Evaluation

At the end of each course, students usually have the opportunity to evaluate the professor's teaching. Frequently this evaluation is conducted by anonymous questionnaire. A summary of the questionnaires is returned to the professor and also becomes a part of the professor's personnel file. Student evaluation of teaching is not without bias. The questionnaire may or may not be reliable or valid for student evaluation of the course as taught. The students may evaluate on the basis of the professor's popularity and on the quantity of work required to pass the course. However, student feedback is just as often useful and enlightening as it is questionable or biased. The professor may wish to make a copy of the evaluation form for each course with any factual notes that might be useful when the evaluation summary is used for input to reappointment, promotion, and/or tenure decisions, as well as for merit recommendations.

Students in some colleges and universities conduct and publish course evaluations to provide information about which courses are "gut" (very easy) courses, which professors are "great" and which should be avoided, etc. With or without such student publications, the students' informal network provides much reliable information about a professor and her courses. Students will often avoid a poor professor or a poor course. Low registration may be a form of student feedback and should be weighed carefully by the professor.

Self-Evaluation

Many professors conduct their own personal evaluations of each course and use the resultant information for course revision. These evaluations are often used to determine how well the professor achieved her own goals for the course and/or for student learning. This information, with some discretion, may also be used in reappointment, promotion and tenure presentations and given to merit and award committees.

A personal in-course evaluation questionnaire should take ten to fifteen minutes to answer. A number of well-tested instruments are nationally available. Questionnaires should address the particular course goals and objectives, classroom presentation, assignments etc. The questions should solicit information about what improvements the students would suggest.

Faculty Evaluation

The committee(s) on reappointment, promotion, and tenure, composed of faculty and, frequently, student representatives, considers the professor's teaching performance. The committee(s) usually look at student evaluations, self evaluations, course syllabi, independent research supervised, new courses offered, and teaching load (the numbers of students enrolled per course per semester). Although a better evaluation of the professor's teaching effectiveness might be obtained years afterward from former students, reappointment, promotion, and tenure decisions are based on information at hand.

Research on Teaching Effectiveness

A large body of research exists on teaching effectiveness. The *Handbook of Research on Teaching* (Wittrock) includes reviews of theoretical, quantitative, and qualitative methodological issues and is particularly comprehensive. Offering any course is essentially an action experiment. Campbell and Stanley have written a classic book titled *Experimental and Quasi-Experimental Designs for Research,* which is very useful for professors considering research on teaching. The conscientious professor is always trying to find new ways to be a more effective teacher and learning manager.

SPECIAL TEACHING-RELATED CONCERNS

Some general societal concerns about education have been addressed in Part I. The special concerns discussed here are particular concerns of the teacher. Cheating and plagiarism are historic concerns. More recently, a litigious society has forced college administrators and faculty to become more sensitive to concerns about legal and affirmative action issues. These concerns include charges of unfair grading, charges of sexual harassment, and charges of racial and ethnic discrimination.

Violations of Academic Ethics: Cheating, Plagiarism, and Fraud

Violations of academic ethical values include cheating, plagiarism, or fraud. The professor bears a responsibility for conveying academia's ethical values—values which are also highly regarded in every democratic society, especially in this so-called Information Age. Cheating and plagiarism are violations of intellectual property. Fraud is intentional misrepresentation or concealment of information.

Intellectual property pertains to original ideas or creative works which belong to their originators in the same way that other property belongs to an owner. Intellectual property refers to the value of knowledge and inspiration; it may not be easily valued in dollars and cents, but it still can be of inestimable worth. Intellectual property is a fuzzy legal area protected by both copyright and patent law. Legal sanctions, referring to the specific form of the original ideas or creative works, are invoked by copyright and patent infringement. Some areas of ideas and methods are sufficiently general and/or fuzzy in their form that copyright and patent infringement would be difficult to prove. A writer, for instance, may borrow someone else's idea but so change the wording that copyright violation could never be proved.

Plagiarism is taking the intellectual property of another person without attributing the ideas and/or wording to their originator. Plagiarism is a common and difficult problem in academia. From the elementary grades onward, students are taught to recapitulate ideas in a text or ideas expressed by a professor. They are often examined and evaluated on their ability to memorize and recapitulate material presented in class. They are seldom taught about plagiarism or about the value of intellectual property, even in high school. No wonder that students become confused about how to differentiate between general knowledge that does not require attribution and specific ideas which are someone's intellectual property. Each scholarly area has particular norms for attributing ideas to their originators, but all areas insist on attribution. The professor must take responsibility for conveying these norms to students and for reinforcing the necessity for them. College and university sanctions for proven violations of intellectual property are severe and can result in suspension or expulsion.

Students may be unaware that ideas taken from a written work must be attributed to their author, whether the material is quoted verbatim or not. However, they know from the elementary level that copying from another student is cheating. Cheating also occurs when a copy of an exam is obtained before it is given or when one student takes an exam in place of another. The student who feels the need to cheat is often over-anxious or academically weak. Such students should be referred for special help, either personal or academic. Ideally, students should not feel the need to cheat. Cheating, like plagiarism, is considered a serious violation of academic ethics and can result in suspension or expulsion.

Professors dislike being put in the position of policing student actions. However, some controls may be necessary to prevent cheating and plagiarism. Control is enhanced by having multiple opportunities to observe the students' work in class, in the laboratory, and on various assignments.

Proctoring in-class tests and examinations to reduce cheating is a common faculty responsibility in most colleges and universities. The current predominance of objective tests and examinations designed to evaluate fact retention and answers to problems may actually encourage cheating. A variation of the objective test requires students to explain or justify their choices for true-false or multiple-choice answers. This evaluates more than the students' ability to memorize facts and makes cheating more difficult. If students' understanding of the subject matter is most effectively evaluated by an objective test or the answer to a problem, rather than by the step-by-step problem solution, two equivalent tests can be given to alternate students. This technique is effective in a crowded classroom where students are seated close to one another.

An alternative to objective tests and exams is the open-book, open-note test or exam where questions are designed to elicit what each individual student has learned about a particular topic. However, the open-book, open-note test lends itself to essay questions. Answers to such questions are difficult and time-consuming to compare and evaluate. The short-answer version of this kind of test is less time consuming to evaluate and still enables the student to express what has been learned in his or her own way.

Cheating and plagiarism outside of class is difficult to detect. The professor must be familiar with a particular source to detect plagiarism in a paper whether the student writes the paper or uses a paper written by a previous student.

Fraud refers to intentional misrepresentation or concealment of information. A student purchasing someone else's paper or paying someone else to write his or her paper is committing fraud. This is not plagiarism because it is paid for or otherwise permitted by the author and, therefore, not a violation of intellectual property; however, the student is fraudulently claiming to have written the paper. Fraud may also occur, for example, in quantitative chemistry when a student records an answer within the acceptable range, even though it was not actually obtained. The recording of the answer is clearly intentional misrepresentation and concealment of the fact that the answer was not actually obtained.

Plagiarism and fraud can also be committed by faculty as well as by students. The publication of fraudulent research data has become an issue in the scientific community. Proof of such fraudulent activity has resulted in the dismissal of tenured faculty. Omitting from a paper information which would damage the conclusions is considered fraudulent behavior. Massaging data so that it appears to be better than it is can also be considered fraudulent behavior. A clear-cut example of fraud as misrepresentation is the professor who represents herself as holding a doctoral degree when, in fact, such a degree was never awarded.

The professor must endeavor to convey acceptable values to her students. Students need to learn these values to interpret their reading and to maintain their integrity in later life, whether in academia, industry, or government. Such values are most effectively conveyed by example, rather than by precept. At the same time, the professor must work to prevent and control plagiarism, cheating, and fraud.

Use of Copyrighted Materials

Intellectual property which is protected by copyright may be copied once for scholarly use. Making multiple copies is illegal under copyright law. The library staff is usually knowledgeable and helpful in providing faculty with guidelines for use of copyrighted material.

Grading

Students have actually litigated against individual faculty members for unsatisfactory or failing grades. Charges of unsatisfactory grading can usually be avoided by a clear grading policy stated in the course syllabus and consistent following of this policy in computing student grades. Written grading policies avoid misunderstanding in the evaluation of papers, tests, and even homework assignments. Some professors tell the class how many students achieved each major grade level at the time a paper, project, test, or exam is returned. Many conscientious professors are able to give individual attention to those students who are working hard but not progressing well. Such professors rarely have problems with accusations about unfair grading.

When questions about a particular student's grade are anticipated, a copy of the student's work should be retained. All interactions with the student should also be documented. The professor may wish to have a questionable project, paper, or exam reviewed by other professors.

Sexual Harassment

Accusations of sexual harassment often occur despite the fact that the person being accused is completely unaware of any actions that might be perceived as harassment. The accused may be completely innocent of intent to sexually harass. Male professors need to be aware that women are especially sensitized to sexual harassment. Professors of both sexes need to be leery of appearing seductive. Professor-student relationships are unequal in power. What the professor intends as ordinary or social may be perceived by the student as unacceptable, unwarranted, and harassing behavior. The student may also believe that such behavior should be accepted as the price for receiving a good grade or passing the course. Charges of sexual harassment, whether from the opposite sex or the same sex, are particularly difficult to handle.

Racial, Ethnic, and Gender Discrimination

Accusations in this area can result from personal biases that the professor may not be aware of. Such biases may be communicated by tone of voice when talking to a student or colleague, by more or less critical attitudes when evaluating a student's efforts, and by body language. The subtleties involved in racial, ethnic, and gender discrimination are as difficult to pinpoint as are the subtleties in sexual harassment. Accusations of racial, ethnic, or gender discrimination can result from perceived unfairness (including the use of jokes and any reference to stereotypes) in any area of professor-student or professor-colleague interaction.

Students from a minority ethnic group, especially those students also coming from a low socio-economic background, may have difficulties with writing or speaking standard English at the college level. Tutoring and remedial services and courses are available to all students on many campuses to bring these basic skills up to acceptable levels.

Gender discrimination occurs from male faculty to female students as well as from faculty of both sexes to students perceived as homosexual. The professor should make a positive effort to use gender-free language and to include examples of women's contributions and of female role models in every course. By the same token, reverse discrimination should be avoided.

Recommendations

These special teaching-related concerns may not occur often, but when they do arise, they take undue amounts of time and emotional energy. Charges of harassment or discrimination may result in the professor's dismissal. The college or university employs staff to stay up to date on current laws which would influence and impact institutional policy and practice. The professor who has questions about any of these concerns is advised to consult with the appropriate college or university lawyers and authorities.

TYPES OF APPOINTMENT

The primary responsibility of most faculty members is stated as effective teaching. Some universities, however, hire researchers and specify in their contracts that teaching will be secondary to the responsibility for research. Some colleges and universities require or allow administrators to teach courses in their discipline in addition to their primary administrative responsibilities. All full-time appointees are expected to serve within the institution and to become involved with student activities, collegial scholarship, and university governance.

Adjunct teaching appointments are usually made in those areas that lack the necessary full-time teaching staff. Often these appointments are in very specialized areas where experience in the field can bring much to the classroom. Adjunct appointees are not required to give service within the college or university; however, such service is generally welcome. Adjuncts should plan to attend departmental faculty meetings when invited and when possible. Adjuncts may be expected to have office hours or to make arrangements to meet with students before and/or after class.

Chapter 14

THE SERVICE ROLE AND ITS RESPONSIBILITIES

The professor functions in a service role within the college or university, the professional community, and the community at large. This role includes responsibilities for advising and supporting student and alumni activities, collegial scholarship, college or university governance, professional societies, continuing education, making presentations, and consulting.

SERVICE WITHIN THE COLLEGE OR UNIVERSITY

The professor is concerned with every aspect of developing and maintaining a high-quality academic program. The uniqueness of each college and university stems, in part, from the general ambience of its setting, its academic programs, and its student activities. This ambience, for the professor, includes scholarly interaction with colleagues and involvement in the various aspects of university governance.

Interaction with Students

Most students want an opportunity to interact closely with their professors both in and outside of class. This interaction is one of the aspects of the higher education experience which prospective students look for, that current students seek, and that graduates remember as an indicator of the quality of their education. The extent of professor-student interaction depends, in part, on the size of the school and the level of the course. Upper classmen and graduate students interact more closely with their professor than do underclassmen who are new to the college or university experience and are not yet focusing on courses in their major field. The extent of the interaction depends, also, upon the college or university administration. In many institutions, faculty participation in advising and steering students during the admissions process has become part of formal administration responsibilities as the institution has grown in size. Some professors will always interact more with students than others, depending on their interests and on their other responsibilities. The difficulty is that the professor could easily spend his full time interacting with students and must balance this responsibility with other demands on his time.

Support of Student Activities

A plethora of student activities is available on every campus. Some of these activities are sponsored by academic departments and/or programs and have faculty advisors working closely with the student group. Faculty advising is particularly important in activities that involve intellectual competition with other colleges and universities in discipline-related events. Other activities in which professors may participate include social service, political action, religious groups, various types of publications, etc. The list of activities is endless.

Student Advising

The importance of mentoring individual student learning has been discussed in other sections of this book as it related to course work and independent research and study. Student advising generally refers to advice about which courses to take and about course sequencing within a particular curriculum. Student advising also refers to consultation about academic difficulties and personal problems.

Quality student advising requires building a relationship with the student being advised. This is not a casual matter. Each student has a unique set of concerns. The student will often wish to discuss career possibilities in the professor's field of interest. Knowledge of course sequences and of current course offerings is important. Some students need advice on building a specially designed course of study for their particular combination of interests.

Young students often seek out a professor with whom they feel comfortable to discuss an academic or personal matter. College may be the first experience that these young students have in living away from home. They are accustomed to having around them a parent or older person with whom they can test their thinking and explore new ideas. The mature student returning to study after a lapse of several years may be concerned about regaining the discipline necessary to study effectively or plan a program of study that will fit in with his or her employment or family responsibilities.

Student advising is a major service responsibility. The professor must learn when a student's academic or personal problems would benefit from referral to trained counselors—either remedial counselors for academic difficulties or psychological and/or medical counselors for more personal difficulties. Each college or university generally has both a written and an unwritten policy concerning student advising. The professor will want to become acquainted with both.

Interaction with students can be very rewarding. The opportunity for such interaction may be part of the reason for choosing an academic career. Interaction which results in a romantic relationship between professor and student may involve considerable risk for both, although some professor-student romances lead to highly successful life-long marriages. Another risky relationship may result from close interaction with the student who flatters the professor into thinking that their relationship can solve some deep-seated psychological dependency or that their relationship will resolve the need for a compassionate parental figure. The fact that many professors enjoy the role of an authority figure simply adds to this risk.

Support of Alumni Activities

Some relationships with students continue after the student graduates and develop into enduring personal friendship. Following a former student's career progress and personal development is one of the rewards of an academic career. Activities where faculty can visit with alumni arise at various college- or university-sponsored events to which both faculty and alumni are invited. A professor may be asked to address an alumni club while working or vacationing away from the college or university. Professional society meetings are also occasions for meeting and visiting with alumni in the same field.

Collegial Scholarship

Scholarly inquiry is the indispensable aspect of the college or university. The notion of collegial scholarship implies the synergy resulting from working together. In the ideal academic community, the professor would find many opportunities for collegial scholarship. In practice, such opportunities may be limited or may slip away.

Informal opportunities for scholarly inquiry may arise during lunch at the faculty club or over a cup of coffee in another professor's office. The professor's teaching will benefit from familiarity with related areas of expertise in teaching and research. Knowing, informing, and sharing are important stimuli for ideas. Discussion of ideas with colleagues can clarify or broaden thinking, lead to suggestions on references or contacts, and generate new fruitful ideas. Sometimes such discussions lead to collaboration on papers, books, or research. Senior professors may seek to bring along junior ones. Junior professors may seek more senior ones when applying for research grants or when needing someone to critique the draft of a paper, etc. Such collegial relationships are more likely to arise within departments. They should be encouraged across departments, especially in related areas. Often such relationships arise as a result of committee work.

Some schools or departments organize faculty retreats devoted to certain content areas rather than to the more usual curricular discussions. Seminars are sponsored for collegial scholarship, especially when a visiting scholar is available. Colloquia may focus on formal or informal presentations of research in progress. Short courses or workshops may be offered to introduce new technology or equipment to the faculty. Professors may audit or take courses from other faculty members as their time permits. Journal clubs can be developed to enable faculty and graduate students to keep up with more literature than any one professor or student can do on an individual basis. Each club member takes responsibility for a set of journals and reports orally or with abstracts to other club members on a regular schedule. Meetings may be arranged to discuss research findings in a particular area.

Universities give lip service to the desirability of interdisciplinary research. In practice, interdisciplinary research needs to be specifically targeted and supported by the institution because it tends to take time away from disciplinary research where the rewards in terms of professional recognition tend to be more obvious. Similar pressures work to encourage individual rather than collaborative work. Single-authored papers and books "count" more than multiauthored ones.

Finally, the formal lectures available on a campus provide yet another opportunity for collegial scholarship, whether these are symposia on specific subjects or presentations by an outside speaker. The academic community is a rich soil for the growth of collegial scholarship, the potential for which is too often unrealized.

College and University Governance

Intrinsic to the concept of academic freedom is a community of scholars making decisions about academic programs. The academic programs are dedicated to the learning of the students through various curricular offerings. In practice, the community of scholars participates in academic decisions by serving on the numerous committees involved in university governance and attending the various meetings that such governance entails.

Faculty Meetings: Governance matters that affect the faculty as a whole are discussed at faculty meetings. These meetings may occur at convocations, often at the beginning of an academic year, where the president of the college or university presides. In some institutions, the faculty may meet as an assembly presided over by an elected moderator. In large universities, representatives of the faculty may meet as a faculty senate. Typical business matters at a faculty meeting may include discussion of reports from the college or university president, reports from institution-wide committees, discussion and approval of new courses and curricula, and various policies relating to academic programs. The faculty may also meet at purely ceremonial occasions such as graduations and the installation of a new college or university president.

Faculty meetings also occur within the separate colleges of a university as well as within individual departments and/or academic programs The structure, level, and governance of faculty meetings varies so greatly from one college or university to another that generalizations about their nature are difficult.

Committees: The structure, level, and scope of college and university committees varies as greatly as the structure and level of faculty meetings. Committees focus on student, faculty, and/or administrative concerns. The college or university governance structure usually includes standing committees and ad hoc committees whose membership may be elective, appointive, or a combination of both. Task forces are developed for major projects. The list of faculty committees is varied and endless.

The typical professor spends time serving on a variety of faculty committees. Some committees enable the professor to become acquainted and to work with faculty outside of a particular program or department. Scheduling meeting time, taking minutes, reading committee materials, drafting documents, participating in lengthy discussions, drafting and debating reports of committee recommendations, presenting recommendations at faculty meetings or to the administration—these are all aspects of committee participation and college and university governance.

Appointment, Promotion and Tenure: Faculty decisions regarding appointment, reappointment, promotion, and tenure are an important aspect of preserving academic freedom. These decisions have been widely accepted within the American higher education community since the American Association of University Professors'

(AAUP) 1915 Declaration of Principles (Joughin). The AAUP exists in part to defend academic freedom. Professors may not be dismissed for arbitrary reasons. Professors are to be evaluated on the basis of teaching ability and scholarly inquiry. They are not to be dismissed because someone disagrees with their ideas or their stand on a particular issue. AAUP policy states that a professor will not be dismissed without a tenure review. Tenure review occurs prior to seven years of service. Tenure denotes a career contract.

This AAUP tenure policy, although protecting academic freedom, has generated other problems. In some colleges and universities where the number of faculty increased as the student body also increased, a subsequent decline in the number of students has led to an oversupply of tenured faculty. Governmental research monies are no longer as available as they were. Tenured professors carried in part by research funding must now be paid with university funds. Costs have escalated and the tenured faculty have aged. A shortage of young faculty is predicted for the turn of the century as limited college and university budgets cannot provide sufficiently high salary levels to attract doctoral graduates to gamble their most productive years on an unpredictable tenuring process.

Colleges and universities have responded to this situation in a variety of ways. Many schools have "tenure-track" positions and "non-tenure-track" appointments. Obviously, the tenure-track positions are the more desirable ones. This two-tier system has enabled schools to control the size of the tenured faculty and at the same time to employ some younger faculty. Some schools have provided generous incentives for early retirement. Many schools have tenure quotas for faculty at the assistant, associate, and full-professor levels.

Each institution has criteria for reappointment, promotion, and tenure. The criteria generally include excellence in teaching, service, research and publications. Few schools grant promotion or tenure to a professor unless the individual has an earned terminal degree (usually a Ph.D. or other doctorate). Outstanding teaching is difficult to evaluate because colleagues seldom attend the classes conducted by the professor. (Evaluation of teaching is discussed in the preceding chapter.) As a result, it seems that undue weight has been placed on scholarly research, particularly publications, in the promotion and tenure process. Evaluation of research is discussed in the next chapter. Evaluation of service is discussed at the end of this chapter. Evaluation of service, like evaluation of teaching, is a difficult matter.

Unfortunately, the promotion and tenure process too often seems capricious. Administrations are constrained by the number of budgetary slots (a quota) for tenured faculty. Therefore, the administration may be forced to focus on an area of teaching, service, or research where the individual's promotion or tenure packet is weak, using this area to justify a negative decision regarding the individual's application for promotion or tenure. A new administrator may change the rules for promotion or tenure which the professor has been following during the term of the new administrator's predecessor. Such changes have too often occurred the year that a professor applies for promotion or tenure. The capricious, overly political nature of the promotion and tenure process, tenaciously defended by the AAUP, has disillusioned many excellent teachers, sending them into jobs where they receive higher salaries and more consistent evaluation of their job performance.

Reappointment, promotion, and tenure decisions are recommended by a departmental committee. The committee's decision must be approved by the departmental dean and his or her superiors, including the college or university president. There may be other steps. The president's decision is usually approved pro forma by the Board of Trustees. There is generally an appeal procedure.

Unions: Many college and university faculties today are represented by a professional union. The two major unions are the National Education Association (NEA) and the American Federation of Teachers (AFT). The American Association of University Professors (AAUP) also represents the faculty in some colleges and universities. Whether or not the faculty is unionized, the supporting staff is usually represented by their own unions. With increasing use of part-time faculty by colleges and universities, unions are working to organize this group whose wages and working conditions are not part of the faculty union contract.

The union acts as a bargaining agent for the employee group's wages and working conditions on the basis that the strength of the union's position lies in the number of its members. Some professors disdain union membership. However, highly educated professionals in many occupations have found that collective bargaining as a union is frequently necessary when such professionals constitute a large employee group within one institution or industry.

SERVICE WITHIN THE PROFESSIONAL COMMUNITY

The professor is actively involved in the scholarly community outside of his college or university. This involvement provides awareness of teaching and research in progress in other places and by other individuals, which gives the professor an opportunity to present his own work and to be active in the field or discipline as a whole. Professional societies provide the major opportunity. Organizations of all kinds welcome addresses and presentations by professors in their areas of expertise. Professorial participation in an invisible college enhances service to the discipline and to the professor's research and publication efforts. The professor may be involved in continuing education activities and conference management. Reviewing or refereeing of books, articles, and grant proposals is an important service responsibility.

Professional Societies

Professional societies exist for virtually every field and subfield of knowledge. Those societies covering broader knowledge areas often have special interest groups that represent subfields, specialized research areas, special areas of practice, or are devoted to special problems. Some professional societies have existed for over 100 years; others have been recently organized.

Members of all professional societies meet at various intervals on local, regional, and national levels to hear contributed papers, special addresses, and to participate in discussions. These meetings also include opportunities to interact informally with colleagues from other institutions. These colleagues may be from other colleges and universities, from research institutions, from industry, or from government. They may be individual practitioners. Getting to know what other people in the field are thinking and doing is important for both teaching and research. Important collaborative efforts often result from these interactions. Larger meetings often have exhibits which enable attendees to peruse the latest publications, newest equipment, and sometimes the newest methods for teaching and/or research in the field. Trade shows may serve a similar purpose. Most professors find that the opportunity to look at the range of new materials presented by a large number of firms at the same time is an efficient method of keeping up and for selecting new materials for classroom or laboratory.

Professional societies provide the professor with an opportunity to serve on the various committees that plan and administer the society's activities. Committee membership is a good way to become acquainted with persons prominent in the field. For the professor who becomes known as a valuable committee member, opportunities arise to chair committees, to organize and moderate meeting sessions, and to run for elective office in the society. Each of these activities can be personally and professionally of great value to the individual who wishes to make a contribution to his field.

Many societies have publication programs. Publications, which are often a benefit of membership in the society, are a means of disseminating information about the society's field of interest. They take the form of scholarly journals, annual reviews of work in the discipline or field, books, tutorials for newly developing areas, proceedings of meetings, directories of members, and newsletters, etc. Society publications provide an important means of keeping up with what is going on in the field. They also are an important place for the professor to publish research findings.

Addresses and Presentations

The professor has many opportunities to speak about research in progress and completed research as well as about opinions on scholarly issues in the field. Such opportunities may include participation in panel discussions, arranging and moderating sessions at professional society meetings, and accepting invitations to address a group of persons interested in his opinions or research. The professor may also seek the opportunity to present material in response to a "call for papers." Calls for papers are general invitations to contribute papers to professional society meetings. A contributed paper may be reviewed for appropriateness and scholarship; responding to a call for papers does not always mean that the paper will be accepted.

The Invisible College

The importance of membership in an invisible college to excellence in teaching and research cannot be overstated. An invisible college is composed of people working and communicating with each other in the same field of knowledge outside of the specific department or college where the professor works. The invisible college is a specialized network which may have an international membership. The professor is in touch with many members of the invisible college on a regular basis by telephone, letter, and electronic mail. The professor turns to his invisible college to find answers to a question, to seek assistance in solving a particular problem, to determine where to locate an obscure document. With the invisible college, the professor is never isolated or without intellectual support. The professor may invest much time in interacting with members of his invisible college, especially if, in a particular subject field, the professor is the only specialist in his college or university. The invisible college is a network of all specialists in that area. Its existence and its value to both teaching and research have been clearly documented.

Continuing Education and Conference Management

Continuing education and conference management both provide opportunities for service in the professional community. Teaching continuing education courses enables the professor to serve practitioners in the field by providing them with up-to-date information about changes and new developments in a particular subject area. These courses are important in technological fields where research is moving rapidly. Some occupations have moved aggressively to deal with obsolescence by requiring periodic continuing education to maintain licensure. Various activities confer continuing education units (CEUs). These activities are usually prescribed by one or more professional societies related to a particular occupation. Continuing education has become "big business" for colleges, universities, professional societies, and for-profit corporations.

Professors who are up to date in their field are often called upon to conduct continuing education courses which vary from one-day workshops to full terms in length. Some colleges and universities now have offices of continuing education which offer a variety of courses and draw from their faculty to design and teach them.

Professors also arrange various conferences and meetings as part of the responsibility of membership in a professional society or as part of their service to their employing institution. These conferences and meetings may be specially funded by a grant from industry, a foundation, or the government. Sometimes members of an invisible college identify an emergent area and arrange a special meeting or conference to focus on the research in this area.

Reviewing and Refereeing

Scholarly manuscripts are critiqued by a peer reviewing and refereeing process before being accepted for publication. Grant proposals are also scrutinized by a similar process.

Book reviewing is an important part of peer reviewing and the publication process. Writing such a review requires a knowledge of other relevant publications in the field. The review should cover not only what is written in the book, but whether or not the book makes a contribution to the field. The review may include comparisons with other similar or related work and usually indicates the reviewer's assessment of why the book should be read and who should read it. Unlike reviewing and refereeing manuscripts and grant proposals, book reviewing is not anonymous. A review is usually signed, giving the reader of the review an indication of the reviewer's bias and level of expertise.

Manuscripts submitted to a scholarly journal are commonly distinguished by the peer review process from those manuscripts submitted to a magazine. An anonymous referee is asked to review the manuscript and determine whether it contributes to knowledge in the field, whether it is appropriate for the particular journal to which it has been submitted, and whether additions or corrections are needed before the manuscript could be accepted for publication. The referee details the positive contributions of the manuscript, notes any errors, and indicates what revisions should be made. Most journals submit a manuscript to several referees. The journal editor makes the final decision to publish or reject the manuscript based on the referees' comments. Manuscripts requiring revision may be reviewed more than once.

Reviewing grant proposals is also anonymous. The reviewer is asked to determine the merit of the proposed work. The reviewer usually bases his or her judgment on a set of criteria specified by the funding agency and on his or her own expertise. After individual reading and evaluation of the various proposals submitted, the reviewers meet as a group to discuss the proposals, reconcile their differences in evaluation, and rank the proposals for funding.

Reviewing and refereeing are significant professorial responsibilities. They ensure that work is of high quality. In reviewing grants, the professor ensures that the funding agency's money is spent in the most fruitful way possible. Judging one's peers is serious and difficult, the more so since the judgments made can positively or negatively affect a colleague's career.

SERVICE WITHIN THE COMMUNITY AT LARGE

Consulting offers the professor the opportunity to solve "real" problems rather than just theoretical ones. Opportunities for consulting vary from field to field. Industry, government, charitable organizations, even other colleges and universities all employ professors as consultants. Consulting broadens teaching by giving many examples that may be used in the classroom. Consulting also supplements college and university salaries.

Professors may be called upon as experts in their fields to lecture to the laity. They may be called upon to testify in court. Depending upon their field, professors may also be asked to serve on various community committees to contribute their expertise.

At the same time, professors may also choose to volunteer their time in areas of interest that do not require their expertise. This involvement and service within the lay community can include service organizations and political groups. Keeping in touch with the concerns of people outside academia helps keep a balance with the "real world." Some professors find their contacts with the real world important for relating to students. Others find these activities provide examples for classroom teaching. Still others just want to broaden their lives beyond academia.

EVALUATION OF SERVICE

Service activities are so varied that the role of service in the professor's performance is difficult to evaluate. Objective comparisons between one professor's level of service and another's are virtually impossible. Deans generally require an annual self-evaluation from each faculty member that lists various service areas as well as accomplishments in teaching and research. Other faculty members both within and outside the department become familiar with the professor by working with the same students, meeting in various scholarly activities, and serving on the same committees.

Other members of the professor's invisible college are probably the best people to determine service and performance within the professional community. Their opinions may or may not be known, solicited, or given weight during the reappointment, promotion, or tenure process.

Service within the lay community carries less weight for reappointment, promotion, or tenure than service within the college, university, and professional communities.

Chapter **15**

RESEARCH
AND PUBLICATION

The twin towers of academia are teaching and research. In general, teaching requires a breadth of knowledge; specialization in a research area adds depth of knowledge in a particular field. The term "research" is used here to include all scholarly inquiry and investigation which might lead to publication. Teaching (or learning management) focuses on synthesizing and communicating new knowledge as it is published. The goal of the learning manager is to guide the leading citizens and scholars of tomorrow by making them aware of knowledge that will influence their lives

Most scholars distinguish between basic research and applied research. Basic research is research for the sake of knowledge. It is often highly specialized, illuminating the unknown and generating new information of interest to a limited group of scientists and graduate students. Applied research builds on the new information and knowledge generated by basic research. It tries to improve our lives and more directly affects our world.

The researcher who teaches can communicate her enthusiasm for research to a group of students, some of whom may become interested in joining this line of either basic or applied research. Sociological research has documented many cases where a professor's enthusiasm for a new area of study has led to an invisible college of geographically scattered students all pursuing further research in the same area and expanding knowledge in the area first "discovered" by their teacher. The professor involved in research or scholarly inquiry clearly brings a greater depth of knowledge to students as well as more current information about the topics she is teaching.

Most professors pursue in-depth scholarship in some aspect(s) of their fields and/or create works that contribute to those fields. This chapter deals with journal and book publication, funded research, intellectual property, and evaluation of research and publication, areas with which the professor may be unfamiliar. There are many other aspects of scholarly work.

INITIAL RESEARCH AND PUBLICATION

The first research goal of every professor must be the earned terminal or doctoral degree. Once this goal is accomplished—hopefully before the professor assumes her first full-time teaching position—the next goal must be to establish a credible record of publication. The beginning professor, planning to teach courses for the first time, has to devote most of her time to teaching; however, research and publication must not be neglected since the professor's publication record is crucial for reappointment, promotion, and tenure.

Some beginning professors with their doctorate in hand are full of ideas for publication and further research while others are less certain about how to proceed. The following suggestions for specific types of publications may prove helpful:
- An article about some aspect of the dissertation
- An essay on a current issue
- An article about research that was set aside earlier
- A book review
- A state-of-the-art review about some aspect of a subject.

Publications that have been reviewed or refereed are most highly regarded. The reviewing or refereeing process is an indicator of quality. Refereed journals are more prestigious than nonrefereed journals. Publication of original research is more highly regarded than reviews of other work.

Once the professor has begun to publish, research efforts must be renewed. Dissertation research can be extended to answer those questions raised by the dissertation research itself. The researcher is now free to pursue the interesting pathways which were not relevant to the focus of the dissertation itself. The professor might wish to develop a new methodological tool for her area of research. Scholarly inquiry resulting from classroom teaching can be a useful and valid area of research. The questions to be asked and answered at the frontiers of knowledge are endless.

PUBLICATION

Presentation of research results for the judgment of peers is the hallmark of scholarship. Preliminary findings, not yet fully analyzed, may be presented at colloquia, seminars or professional meetings. Funded research usually requires periodic progress reports, including preliminary findings. Despite the fact that preliminary findings and sometimes final research results may be widely disseminated, these are not considered "published." Publication in most scientific areas requires submission of research results to refereeing by one's peers. The most stringent and rigorous refereeing occurs in the most prestigious journals or reviews. Research is evaluated by its ability to stand the tests of time and the efforts of others to validate the findings and expand upon them.

In the humanities and some of the social sciences, book publishing (as distinguished from journal article publishing) is the norm. This difference in norms between different areas of knowledge may reflect the fact that books in rapidly moving research areas are obsolete by the time they are published. The difference may also reflect the fact that some scientists deal with smaller and more discrete problems. The difference may even be a matter of style or some other combination of factors. Each new scholar becomes aware of the publishing traditions of her field, learns the prestigious publication media, and the sources of the most important new information.

The publish-or-perish syndrome in academia is real, although it may be unfortunate. The extent to which this syndrome has contributed to the logarithmic growth of published research is unclear. The researcher-professor is well advised to emphasize quality work published in quality journals or by quality publishers. One's publication record will be used often: for every job application, grant application, national committee consideration, promotion, review and, finally, for an obituary.

In the publish-or-perish environment, publication in the lay literature does not "count" and is often frowned upon. Comments in trade publications do not count either, although they provide exposure which may result in paid consultation. Commercial success fattens the pocketbook, but has questionable value for reappointment, promotion, and tenure.

Procedure for Publication of a Journal Article

The following are the steps to be taken for publication in a journal of the professor's particular field:

• Have a senior colleague review the completed manuscript for comments.

• Revise the manuscript.

• Decide on a publication source (e.g., a journal) and revise the manuscript according to the style of that source. Criteria for contributions and instructions are available in journals and from publishers.

• Devise an informative title for readers who will be scanning the publication's table of contents or retrieving the article from an abstracting and indexing source.

• Write an informative abstract, as appropriate.

• Submit the manuscript to a publication source.

• Revise the manuscript according to referee comments or send it to another suggested source.

• After an article is accepted, retain data on which the article was based for as long as readers may raise questions about it—for at least seven years, possibly indefinitely. Drafts, on the other hand, may be discarded, but be careful about discarding them if the article has multiple authorship.

• Review and edit the galleys carefully, taking special care with numbers and tables. A psychiatric textbook had to be recalled from the bookstores because an error in placing a decimal point in a drug dosage resulted in a lethal dose!

• Respond promptly to the editor's questions; return galleys quickly.

• Should a prestigious journal invoke a page charge (a not uncommon practice), the author is expected to have grant or university funds to cover this charge.

Book Publishing

The process of publishing a book is lengthy. Most publishers work from a prospectus. A prospectus is a proposal for a book that usually contains an approximate table of contents, a typical chapter, and the justification or need for the book. The decision about whether to encourage the writing of the book will vary depending on how well known the author is to the publisher.

Publishers often have different divisions, each of which focuses on a particular type of book. The textbook division may even be divided into levels of education. Textbook publishing decisions are based on the perceived market and are driven by marketing considerations. Scholarly books, on the other hand, rarely have sufficient demand to make money for the publisher, much less the author. Therefore, commercial publishers rarely publish scholarly books. These are left to the publication programs of societies and of university presses which have an institutional mission as not-for-profit organizations to produce scholarly works. The commercial publishing house would like to produce tens of thousands of copies of a book, where the society or university press may be willing to consider producing only a few thousand copies.

Editors and publishers usually attend professional society meetings and enjoy meeting prospective authors. A prospective author may also obtain an introduction from colleagues who have worked with a particular publisher. Publishers will seek out well-known scholars for books in areas for which they perceive a market interest. The prospectus provides a basis for discussion of the proposed book. The publisher may refer the prospectus to his or her book editor and perhaps to outside editorial consultants. The book contract which may result often is written on a form standard to the trade.

In the standard contract, the author's royalties will be a percentage of the cost per copy of the book, after a minimum number of copies have been sold. The percentage increases with the number of copies sold. The standard contract will usually contain a clause specifying a date by which the manuscript will be submitted. Most publishers turn the manuscript over to an editor who will work with the author to make any revisions and who will then oversee the publication process.

An author must be prepared to spend a lot of time in preparing the completed manuscript for publication. Comments and criticism from friends and colleagues may result in minor, even major revision. Copyright releases and other permissions must be obtained to use restricted manuscripts, quotes and figures, tables and pictures. Illustrations must be prepared. Figures and tables must be formatted. The introduction and/or preface, the table of contents, and index must all be prepared. Decisions about typography and page layout must be made. Galleys and page proofs must be carefully reviewed. Limited changes can be made in the galleys; only essential changes should be made to page proofs. The publisher and the author work together to send initial copies of the completed book to appropriate reviewing sources.

FUNDED RESEARCH

This section should be considered as a brief overview of a very large, complex, and ever-changing area. The professor is advised to use this overview only as a starting point to seek expert assistance from specially designated college or university staff.

Researchers with substantial funding can usually exchange teaching time for research time. Some professors have research appointments rather than teaching appointments. The professor with a research appointment continues with the university only as long as salary can be supported by the research grants and/or contracts with which she is involved.

Funding is required for research which would require specific space, equipment, support personnel, large amounts of computer time, etc. Funding may also be required for research involving travel. Both direct costs and indirect (overhead) costs must be included in funding proposals. Overhead costs can add a considerable amount to the direct costs of the research itself.

Funding Sources

• *In-house Funding*: Colleges and universities have limited funds to support small research projects, computer time, publication and printing costs. Deans or department chairmen may also be able to approve a reduction in teaching load to support a professor's research efforts.

• *Government Funding*: Federal, state, and local government agencies award both grants and contracts for research and services. Interested persons, both professors and persons from industry, regularly visit and maintain contact with governmental sources to learn about forthcoming Requests for Proposals (RFPs) and about what the funding agency is actually looking for in responses to an RFP. Grant proposals are reviewed by a panel appointed by the funding agency. Contracts are generally awarded in open, competitive bidding.

• *Foundation Funding:* Foundations have specific missions and interests. Funds are awarded along the lines of these interests to researchers whose work is known to the foundation and who can be counted on to further the mission and interests of the foundation.

• *Corporate Funding:* Corporations usually fund some in-house research devoted to developing new products and to improving existing ones. Large corporations also have programs for funding college and university research in areas of their particular interest.

• *Fellowships:* Colleges and universities, governmental agencies, corporations and foundations are all sources for fellowships for research and study. Fellowships are awarded to undergraduates as well as to holders of doctoral degrees for post-doctoral study.

Most colleges and universities have designated staff to investigate funding sources for students and professors. The professor who works with this staff can significantly increase the probability of obtaining funds for research.

Proposal Writing

Proposals for funded research are similar to those for dissertation research but usually much less elaborate. They usually contain the following sections:
- Statement of problem and/or need for the research project;
- Proposed work statement, including a time frame;
- Review of related research;
- Budget, including direct and overhead costs;
- Capabilities of the principal investigator and others who will work on the project.

Proposals should be long enough to cover the subject and short enough to be interesting—rarely longer than 20 pages. Grants officers will immediately discard proposals which do not respond to their needs or which have not been delivered on time.

A large, readily available literature exists on writing proposals and obtaining grants. The college or university staff member in charge of grants and contracts will also provide the new researcher with general assistance and specific instructions. This staff member will frequently help with the budget page and often see that the correct approvals and signatures are obtained. The professor should inquire about funding cycles. For instance, an RFP may be announced in late November with proposals due in early January to be reviewed in April for awards to be made in July to be funded in October. The usual short time period between the announcement of the RFP and the due date for the proposal indicates the need for being constantly and personally in touch with possible funding sources. In addition to inquiring about funding sources, the professor should also find out about the time required for the college or university approval process. This approval process can frequently take two weeks before all the required signatures are obtained. Finally the professor should know that late proposals, even those only five minutes late, are generally discarded. For this reason many professors will hand-carry their proposals or use a courier service to insure that their proposals arrive in good time.

Proposal writing is a thankless, too often fruitless task. Competition for funds is keen, and funding for research is tight. Proposals may be approved but never funded because of budgetary constraints. Budget constraints may also unexpectedly reduce the amount of funding for a research project before it is ever completed. Proposal writing should be considered in parallel with other research activities, whether funded or not.

PROTECTION OF RESEARCH RESULTS AND PUBLICATION RIGHTS

Copyrights and patents are the most common means of protecting researcher's results or writing from unauthorized use by other persons or corporations. Trademarks and service marks are similar forms of protecting the results of intellectual creativity from pirating by others. To the scholar, the writings or discoveries produced by her scholarship are as valuable as any personal property. This intellectual property represents a major investment in time, effort, and, often, money. Intellectual property (copyrights and patents, trademarks and servicemarks) can be bought and sold.

While writing and research can be protected by copyright and patent, these protections can be infringed upon. One common infringement is plagiarism. Plagiarism is quoting, or using ideas or language nearly like that of another person without giving credit to or getting permission from that person. Essentially, plagiarism is stealing. The word actually derives from the Latin *plagiarius* meaning kidnapper.

In academia, the penalties for plagiarism are severe. Plagiarism may result in dismissal from a college or university. The professor dismissed for plagiarism will have difficulty obtaining another academic appointment and/or grant funding. Plagiarism of research data is a topic of increasing concern within the academy.

Copyright

The 1976 U.S. Copyright Act applies to original works authored in any tangible medium of expression. These media include books, periodicals, computer programs, musical compositions, choreography, motion pictures, sculpture, audio recording, etc. Any author is entitled to apply for copyright protection. This protection gives the copyright owner exclusive rights to the work, including reproduction and distribution. In general, copyright protection lasts from the time of creation of the work until 50 years after the death of the author.

The major exception to obtaining permission from the author(s) to use their work allows scholars to copy part of a copyrighted work *one time only* for "fair use." Systematic copying for classroom use and copying the whole work are, by law, not permitted.

Notice of copyright is required and consists of the word "copyright," the symbol © or the abbreviation "copr.," the year of first publication, and the name of the owner. For example: Copyright 1989 John Smith. Copyright forms and information can be obtained from the Information Section LM-455, Copyright Office, The Library of Congress, Washington, DC 20559.

In practice, most journals require copyright release before publishing articles. (This may mean that the professor must obtain a copyright release to reproduce her own graph.) Obviously, written copyright release must be obtained before publishing material that was written by someone else, even with attribution. Release of copyright has no financial implications for an author publishing in a scholarly journal. In any publication where royalties might be important, consult a lawyer before releasing copyright.

Patents

Patent law has a constitutional basis. The purpose of a patent is to encourage commercial manufacturing and production by giving exclusive right to an invention for a certain period of time, after which it goes into the public domain. For example, Bayer obtained a patent on aspirin that has now expired. Today, aspirin is in the public domain. A customer must now ask specifically for "Bayer aspirin," if this is the brand desired. Patented inventions are generally available upon payment to the manufacturer or inventor.

Obtaining a patent is a lengthy and specialized process, usually requiring the services of a patent lawyer. Many colleges and universities and most corporations have a patent policy giving the institution the ownership of any patents produced by its employees.

EVALUATION OF RESEARCH AND PUBLICATION

Research and publication are easier to evaluate than teaching or service. Research can be evaluated more or less objectively in terms of the judgment of one's peers and, in the case of funded research, in terms of the dollars brought into the college or university. The reputation of every college and university is enhanced by the amount and level of research with which its faculty is involved, which adds to the importance of research in evaluating a professor's total performance from an administrator's point of view. From a student's point of view, the professor involved with research may or may not be a superior teacher or manager of student learning, but can certainly bring new and up-to-date information about her area of research to the classroom.

The most prestigious research studies contribute validated original thinking to a specific field. Replication or validation or further development based on the research studies of others is important in the advancement of knowledge, but has less prestige. Unless new theories are accompanied by data to verify them, they are often less well-received than data-based studies extending accepted theoretical work. Prospective longitudinal studies are neglected since studies having shorter time frames build the researcher's reputation more quickly. The importance of reviews, especially state-of-the-art reviews, is often neglected. Opinion pieces may or may not be considered as contributions to research. The publish-or-perish syndrome too often emphasizes the number of a professor's publications rather than the quality of her research or publications. However, limits on publications considered for promotion or tenure may return the focus to quality of research rather than quantity of publications.

Quality is evaluated by peer review and refereeing and by the frequency with which a researcher's work is cited by other researchers over a time period. New research is always cited more frequently than older research. High-quality research tends to be cited over a longer time period than research with limited scope or of lesser quality. Evaluation of research is built into the cultural norms of academia. The relative ease with which quality research can be measured explains why research tends to be valued as a professor-researcher performance measure more highly than the value placed on teaching (learning management) or service.

APPENDIX A

Summary of the Taxonomies of Educational Objectives*
A Classification of Educational Goals

I.   THE COGNITIVE DOMAIN

    1.00   Knowledge

        1.10   Knowledge of specifics

            1.11 Knowledge of terminology

            1.12 Knowledge of specific facts

        1.20   Knowledge of ways and means of dealing with specifics

            1.21 Knowledge of conventions

            1.22 Knowledge of trends and sequences

            1.23 Knowledge of classifications and categories

            1.24 Knowledge of criteria

            1.25 Knowledge of methodology

        1.30   Knowledge of the universals and abstractions in a field

            1.31 Knowledge of principles and generalizations

            1.32 Knowledge of theories and structures

    2.00   Comprehension

        2.10   Translation

        2.20   Interpretation

        2.30   Extrapolation

    3.00   Application

    4.00   Analysis

        4.10   Analysis of elements

        4.20   Analysis of relationships

        4.30   Analysis of organizational principles

5.00 Synthesis

    5.10 Production of a unique communication

    5.20 Production of a plan, or proposed set of operations

    5.30 Derivation of a set of abstract relations

6.00 Evaluation

    6.10 Judgments in terms of internal evidence

    6.20 Judgments in terms of external criteria

II. THE AFFECTIVE DOMAIN

1.0 Receiving (Attending)

    1.1 Awareness

    1.2 Willingness to receive

    1.3 Controlled or selected attention

2.0 Responding

    2.1 Acquiescence in responding

    2.2 Willingness to respond

    2.3 Satisfaction in response

3.0 Valuing

    3.1 Acceptance of a value

    3.2 Preference for a value

    3.3 Commitment

4.0 Organization

    4.1 Conceptualization of value

    4.2 Organization of a value system

5.0 Characterization by a Value or Value Complex

    5.1 Generalized Set

    5.2 Characterization

* *Taxonomy of Educational Objectives: The Classification of Educational Goals. Handbook 1: Cognitive Domain,* Bloom, Benjamin S. et al. (eds.), David McKay, New York, 1956 and *Handbook 2: Affective Domain,* Krathwohl, David R. et al. (eds.), David McKay, New York, 1964.
Extracted from the appendices by permission of the publisher.

APPENDIX B
A Syllabus Checklist

1. Course number, title, and instructor's name

2. Course goals and objectives
   Define the specific knowledge, skills, and/or tasks which the
   student will be expected to acquire upon completion of the course

3. Requirements
   Prerequisite courses and/or knowledge required for enrollment
      in the course
   Textbook(s) required for the course. Include price, where
      possible
   Other materials and/or supplies which the student must purchase
      for use in the course
   Other relevant requirements

4. Assignments, papers and projects
   Specify type and quantity of homework
   Describe briefly the paper(s) and/or projects which must be
      completed
   Describe briefly any other assignments which will be required
      for the course

5. Sequence of topics to be covered
   Prefer a class-by-class schedule
   Include due-dates for major reviews, tests, exams, term
      papers/projects

6. Attendance and grading policy
   Define attitude toward student attendance
   Define criteria, if any, for make-up and/or extra-credit work
   Specify weight (%) of each component (homework, tests, exam,
      projects) used to calculate final course grade
   Include conversion scale used, where necessary, between
      numeric and letter grades

7. Instructor's office hours

   Specify office location, telephone and a regular time students can call and/or confer

   For adjunct instructors, provide a means of contact for students, outside of class

8. Bibliography and/or additional list of readings and course-related materials students can consult on their own

REFERENCES

Anderson, S. B., Ball, Samuel, Murphy, R. T. & Asssoc., *Encyclopedia of Educational Evaluation: Concepts and Techniques for Evaluating Education and Training Programs*, Jossey-Bass, San Francisco, 1975.

APLET [Association for Programmed Learning and Educational Technology] *Yearbook of Educational and Instructional Technology*, 1976/77—

Beard, Ruth M. and Hartley, James, *Teaching and Learning in Higher Education*, 4th Ed., Harper & Row, London, 1984.

Berkson, I. B. *The Ideal and the Community*, Harper & Bros, New York, 1958.

Bloom, Allan *The Closing of the American Mind*, Simon & Schuster, New York, 1987.

Brown, George and Atkins, Madeleine *Effective Teaching in Higher Education*, Methuen, London, 1988.

Campbell, Donald T. and Stanley, Julian C., *Experimental and Quasi-Experimental Designs for Research*, Rand McNally, Chicago; Reprinted from *Handbook of Research on Teaching*, 1963.

Collins, Michael J. "Moral judgment and college curricula," in Young, Robert E. and Eble, Kenneth E. (eds.), *College Teaching and Learning: Preparing for New Commitments, New Directions for Teaching and Learning*, no. 33, Spring 1988, pp 21-30.

Copyright Office, Library of Congress. *Copyright Basics*, U.S. Government Printing Office, 1988-202-135/60,046.

Dunkin, Michael J. with the assistance of Barnes, Jennifer, "Research on Teaching in Higher Education," in: *Handbook of Research on Teaching*, 3rd Ed., Merlin C. Wittrock, (ed.), MacMillan, New York, 1986, pp 754-777.

Eble, Kenneth E. *The Craft of Teaching: A Guide to Mastering the Professor's Art*, 2nd Ed., Jossey-Bass, San Francisco, 1988.

Ericksen, Stanford C. *The Essence of Good Teaching,* Jossey-Bass, San Francisco, 1984.

Estes, William K. *Models of Learning, Memory and Choice: Selected Papers,* Praeger, New York, 1982.

Gardner, Howard *The Mind's New Science: A History of the Cognitive Revolution,* Basic Books, New York, 1985, 1987.

Guide to Effective Teaching, Change Magazine Press, New York, 1978.

Guilford, J. P. "Intelligence has three facets," *Science* 160:615-620, 10 May, 1968.

Guskey, Thomas R. *Improving Student Learning in College Classrooms,* Charles C Thomas, Springfield, IL, 1988.

Handbook of Research on Teaching, 3rd Ed., Merlin C. Wittrock, (ed.), MacMillan, New York, 1986.

Janssen, Peter, "Undergraduate TAs: Motivated and well prepared," in: *Guide to Effective Teaching,* Change Magazine Press, New York, 1978. pp 65-67.

Joughin, Louis, (ed.), "The 1915 Declaration of Principles" in: *Academic Freedom and Tenure: A Handbook of the American Association of University Professors,* Univ. of Wisconsin Press, Madison, WI, 1969, pp 157-176.

Mayer, Robert F. *Preparing Instructional Objectives,* David S. Lake Pub., Belmont, CA, 1984.

Nash, Laura L. "The rhythms of the semester," in: Gullette, Margaret Morganroth, *The Art and Craft of Teaching,* Harvard-Danforth Center for Teaching and Learning, Cambridge, MA, 1982, pp 70-87.

Nisbett, Richard E., Fong, Geoffrey T., Lehman, Darrin R. and Cheng, Patricia W. "Teaching reasoning," *Science* 238:625-651, 30 Oct., 1987.

Pintrich, Paul R. "Student learning and college teaching," in: Young, Robert E. and Eble, Kenneth E. (eds.) *College Teaching and Learning: Preparing for New Commitments, New Directions for Teaching and Learning,* no 33, Spring 1988, pp 71-86.

Segerstrale, Ullica "The multifaceted role of the section leader," in: Gullette, Margaret Morganroth (ed.), *The Art and Craft of Teaching,* Harvard-Danforth Center for Teaching and Learning, Cambridge, MA, 1982, pp 49-69.

Scott, Anne Firor "Why I teach by discussion," in: Deneef, A. Leigh, Goodwin, Craufurd D. and McCrate, Ellen Stern, *The Academic's Handbook,* Duke Univ. Press, Durham, NC, 1988, pp 141-145.

Sternberg, Robert J. "Integration: questions and answers about the nature and teaching of thinking skills," in: Baron, J. B. and Sternberg, R. J. *Teaching Thinking Skills: Theory and Practice*, W. H. Freeman, 1987, p 252.

Sternberg, Robert J. *The Triarchic Mind: A New Theory of Human Intelligence*, Viking Press, New York, 1988.

Taxonomy of Educational Objectives: The Classification of Educational Goals. Handbook 1: Cognitive Domain, Bloom, Benjamin S. et al. (eds.), David McKay, New York, 1956 and *Handbook 2: Affective Domain*, Krathwohl, David R. et al. (eds.), David McKay, New York, 1964.

Waldrop, M.M. "Toward a unified theory of cognition," *Science* 241:27-29, 1 July, 1988 and "Soar: a unified theory of cognition," *Science* 241:296-298, 15 July, 1988.

Westmeyer, Paul *Effective Teaching in Adult and Higher Education*, Charles C Thomas, Springfield, IL, 1988.

Whitehead, Alfred North *The Aims of Education*, Mentor, New York, 1949.

INDEX

by Joy K. Moll